STILL ALIVE
BUT AT WHAT COST

BURKE BRYANT

Dedications

THIS BOOK IS DEDICATED to Sharlene Bryant, a mother whose love and strength shaped me into the person I am today. Despite my fiery temper as a child, she always knew how to guide, teach, and love me unconditionally. I miss her every day, love her deeply, and carry her with me in everything I do.

It is also dedicated to those who served before me, beside me, and long after me—men and women who spend their lives quietly mending the broken and carrying the vulnerable, asking nothing in return. Their steadfast compassion is a gift to a world that desperately needs it.

To EOD Christopher "Swampy" Garrett—a husband, a father, a skilled explosives expert who gave his life serving strangers—you are deeply missed, brother.

And to the ones in the shadows—behind keyboards, in encrypted chat rooms, operating alone under call signs—providing the intelligence that keeps ground teams safe, guides rescue operations, delivers supplies, and sustains missions. You know who you are. This is for you.

To every single donor who has stood with us—thank you. Without your support, none of this work would have been possible. You have been our lifeline, our steady hand in the chaos, the reason we can step into danger and bring people home. I see you. I feel your impact. I am deeply grateful. Thank you for being part of this mission.

Forward

I'VE KNOWN THE AUTHOR of this book in two capacities that rarely overlap cleanly: as a colleague I trusted with real responsibility and leadership, and as a friend I watched carry more than most people ever see. In professional settings, this was someone you wanted beside you when things went sideways. clear-headed under pressure, disciplined, relentless about mission and standards. He understood risk, accepted it without drama, and made decisions others hesitated to make. In personal moments, that same drive rarely switched off, but it revealed an added thoughtfulness that wasn't always visible to those who only knew him at work. Momentum wasn't just a way of operating; it was a way of being in the world.

As a colleague, I recognize the professionalism and seriousness that run through these pages. The precision, restraint, and refusal to exaggerate will feel familiar to anyone who has served alongside people like him. As a friend, I recognize the courage it took to write them. This is not a story of retreat or regret. It is the story of someone redefining strength on his own terms, with clarity and intention rather than force, and with the discipline to question assumptions that once went unchallenged.

For a long time, that momentum looked like strength to everyone around him. It certainly did to me. He endured, adapted, absorbed, and kept moving forward. In environments where hesitation could cost lives, that quality mattered. It still does. But what this book makes clear - what I don't think even he fully understood at the time - is how easily endurance can become a hiding place. Not from danger, but from reflection. Not from failure, but from the quieter cost of never stopping long enough to take stock of what is being carried forward.

This is not a book about heroics in the way people usually expect. Those moments are here, and they are real, but they are not the point. The point is what happens after the noise fades, after the urgency dissolves, and the only thing left is the accumulated weight of years spent pushing past internal signals that something needs attention. As someone who walked alongside him through parts of that journey, I can say this reckoning did not come easily - and it did not come all at once.

It unfolded slowly, often uncomfortably, and required a kind of honesty that is far rarer than bravery under fire.

What you are about to read is rare precisely because it refuses the familiar arc. There is no triumph neatly tied up at the end, no simple redemption through more effort or harder work. Instead, there is accountability - honest, unsparing, and inward-facing. The author confronts a truth many in high-performance, service-driven worlds quietly avoid: that survival and success can coexist with erosion, and that being effective is not the same as being whole

Readers will find in this book not a set of answers, but a model of responsibility that is seldom discussed - the responsibility to remain whole, even when systems reward the opposite. Burke's journey reminds us that coming home is not a single moment, and that stopping is not failure. Sometimes, it is the most disciplined and necessary choice a person can make.

I know the man who wrote these words. This book reflects him accurately—not just as he was in motion, but as he is now: attentive, grounded, and finally willing to listen.

— Hels Goeth
Investigative Journalist

Author's Note

E VERY STORY IN THIS book is true—as true as memory allows.

The timelines have been compressed. The chaos distilled. Some operations took days, others stretched over weeks or months. In reality, these missions weren't back-to-back. They spanned over two decades—each one separated by time, geography, and moments too complex to squeeze between chapters.

But what's written here captures the core. The pressure. The consequence. The cost. Both physical and mental.

Not every mission made it in. If they had, this book would be thick enough to stop a bullet. What you're holding are the ones that stuck. The ones that changed me. The ones I still wake up remembering. The ones that left dirt under my nails and blood in the seams of who I am.

For the safety of those involved—the people beside me, the ones we tried to save, and even those we couldn't—I've changed names. The same goes for the organizations. This world doesn't always forgive, and some truths are better left untraceable.

Some of the characters in this book were crafted to help carry the weight of the lessons learned—composites drawn from real moments and real people. I shaped them to better explore the complexities of loss, emotion, struggle, and survival in a way that served the story and respected those who lived it.

This isn't a hero's story. It's not a redemption arc. It's a slow bleed of memory and aftermath—a raw record of what happens when you step into places most people run from. Not perfectly. Not always successfully. But honestly.

If you're looking for clean endings, skip ahead.

This is the grit. The wreckage. The human cost.

These are the stories that stayed.

And this is me, finally letting them breathe.

-Burke Bryant

Prologue

THERE ARE MOMENTS WHEN everything slows down.

Not in a dramatic way. Not the way people think. It's quieter than that. The noise drops out and what's left gets sharp. You notice things you shouldn't have time to notice—the way dust hangs in the air, the sound of someone trying not to panic, your hands moving before you've finished thinking.

That's where I learned to live.

By the time most people were running away, I was already moving toward it. Earthquakes. Floods. War zones. Places where nothing was stable and nothing was guaranteed. I went because I could help. That was the reason. It wasn't wrong.

There are people alive because we got there in time. I still see some of their faces. Not all of them—just the ones that stuck. The ones that don't fade no matter how much time passes. The ones who looked at you like you were the difference between making it and not.

We saved a lot of people. That part is true.

I built my life around that feeling. Urgency. Purpose. Being needed *right now*. When everything depends on what you do in the next few seconds, there's no room for anything else. No past. No future. Just the next move.

It's a clean way to live.

Cleaner than staying still.

Because when things got quiet, everything I wasn't dealing with was still there. Waiting. Grief doesn't go anywhere just because you keep moving. It just waits until you stop.

So I didn't stop.

There was always another call. Another place. Another reason to go. And at some point, I stopped asking why. It stopped being a question.

It just became what I did.

I missed things.

Not small things. Not things you can circle back to later. The kind that don't wait. The kind that matter whether you show up or not.

I wasn't there when my mother died.

There are explanations for that. Distance. Timing. Being on the other side of the world when it happened. All of that is true.

But it's not the whole truth.

The truth is, I had built a life where not being there was normal. Leaving was normal. Staying was the exception. I didn't think about it like that at the time. I didn't think about it at all.

I knew how to work in chaos. I knew how to make decisions when things were falling apart. I knew how to keep people alive when it didn't look possible.

I didn't know how to sit still.

I didn't know how to deal with something I couldn't fix. I didn't know how to be there for the people in my own life without turning it into a problem to solve or something to avoid.

That catches up with you.

Eventually the calls slow down. Or you do. The urgency that used to find you everywhere starts to thin out. And then there's space where it used to be.

And that's when everything you pushed aside starts to show up.

This isn't a book about disasters.

Those are part of it, but they're not the point. The point is what a life like that does to you. What it gives you, and what it takes without asking. The things you don't notice you're losing until they're already gone.

I didn't want to write this.

Because writing it means staying still long enough to be honest about what it cost.

Not just what I did.

But what I avoided.

1

Sharlene

S HE HAD ONE JOB her entire adult life. Got it straight out of high school and kept it until they gave her a plaque and a retirement party and sent her home to the life she'd been building toward for forty years. Executive banker. Same desk, same institution, same steady accumulation of everything that was supposed to matter — savings, security, a number in an account that said *you will be okay, you will be fine, you have enough.*

I was not that.

I was the kid who ran. Not from her — or not only from her — but from everything that felt like it was trying to nail me down. Responsibility. Routine. The idea that a good life meant the same thing every day until it didn't. I lived like the ground beneath me was temporary, which it usually was, and I didn't see anything wrong with that. She did. She had every right to.

I was a bad seed for a long time. I won't dress that up. I ran toward edges. I avoided the things I was supposed to do and chased the things I wasn't supposed to want. She watched that and made her calculations and I can't blame her for what she concluded. The evidence supported it.

But somewhere around twenty-one something shifted. Not in how I lived — I was still running — but in why. The running started to have a direction. Every new thing I chased, every pivot, every leap toward something different was pointed at the same destination: her approval. I wanted her to look at what I was doing and say *yes, that, that's the one.* I wanted to find the version of myself she could be proud of and stay there.

The problem was I could never tell when I'd missed. She didn't say much when something fell short. She just went quiet in a particular way, or asked a practical question that contained the real question inside it — *but how does that work financially?* — and I'd feel the distance open up again and I'd move on. Try something else. Find the next thing that might finally be the thing.

It went on like that for years. Undercover work. Journalism. Military. War reporting. Different shapes of the same restlessness, each one a new attempt to build something she could point to. I was never consciously thinking *I'm doing this for her.* But looking back I can see the pattern clearly. Every time I sensed I was falling short in her eyes I ran to the next thing. And then the next. And then the next.

Then I was in my thirties and I started the humanitarian work and something changed. The operations. The disaster zones. The strangers pulled from floodwater and carried through rubble. She heard about it and something in her shifted too. She said it out loud, once or twice — *I'm proud of you.* Words I had been chasing for most of my adult life.

I didn't know what to do with them.

By then I was calloused in ways I hadn't fully accounted for. I'd been running so long, adjusting so many times, absorbing so many quiet disappointments, that when the words finally came I couldn't receive them cleanly. I turned them over instead. Examined them. Wondered what they meant. Was it real pride — the kind that comes from actually seeing someone and recognizing what they've built? Or was it something else? Had she simply reached the point of surrender? Had she been trying to reach me for so long that she'd finally decided *I'm proud of you* was easier than continuing to wait for something she recognized?

I don't know. I never asked. And now I can't.

That uncertainty is its own kind of weight. It would have been simpler, in a way, if she'd never said it. Silence is at least honest. But *I'm proud of you* spoken by someone who might have just given up — that lives in you permanently unresolved. You can't hold it as comfort and you can't set it down as loss. It just sits there, in between, asking a question that has no answer anymore.

The cancer came the way it comes — quietly at first, then in waves. One type, then another, then another. Ten years of it. She fought it the way she did everything — with discipline, with the particular stubbornness of a woman who had decided early that life required endurance and had built herself accordingly. She kept her routines as long as she could. She managed her affairs. She was not a person who fell apart.

And then, eventually, she stopped fighting. Not because she lost — because she decided. That's the part I've had to sit with. She made a choice. After ten years of one thing and then another and then another, she decided she was done. I understand that more than I want to.

She died while I was in Florida. Not on a mission. Not in a war zone or a flood zone or anywhere that would have made the distance make sense. Just Florida. Present in my own life for once, ordinary, unremarkable. And she left anyway.

My sister called. Said it simply, the way you say things when the weight of them is too much for elaboration. I sat with the phone in my hand after she hung up and didn't move for a long time.

I didn't go to the funeral.

I've never fully explained that to anyone. I'm not sure I can explain it now. What I know is that the wall I'd built — the one that kept me moving forward, that kept grief at a distance, that let me function in places where functioning was the difference between life and death — that wall didn't come down for funerals. It didn't come down for the things that would hurt me most. That was the point of it.

I told myself I couldn't go. I didn't tell anyone that I'd made that choice. I just didn't go and I let the absence speak for itself and I tried to spend that day not thinking about what was happening without me.

Then someone told me it was streaming. For those who couldn't make it.

I watched my mother's funeral alone on a screen. I watched the people who loved her gather around her without me. I watched the rituals of grief play out in a room I should have been standing in. And somewhere in the middle of it the wall came down, just enough, and I broke. Sitting alone in a room watching a screen, crying in a way I hadn't let myself cry in years.

I had failed her again. That's what it felt like. One more time, at the moment that mattered most, I had found a way to not be there.

I don't know what the family thought. I've wondered. I've never asked.

What I know is this: she said she was proud of me. Once or twice, near the end. I heard the words and I couldn't trust them and now I will spend the rest of my life not knowing whether that was real or whether she had simply run out of other things to say.

I hope it was real.

I'm still not sure.

2

Gut Punch

THE CELL SMELLED LIKE piss and sweat. No windows. One bare bulb. The woman in the corner hadn't looked away since the door slammed shut.

She had killed her husband the night before.

At least that's what the guards told me after they threw me inside.

She was high on heroin—still high, by the look of it. Pupils blown black, body sagging against the wall but strung tight underneath—like something about to snap. Sweat ran off her in streams, sharp and sour. When I stepped inside, she locked on me. Didn't blink. Didn't look away. Just stared with those dead black eyes, breathing shallow, each breath sour and wrong.

It wasn't curiosity. It was something colder.

This wasn't just any jail. It was a holding cell outside Juba, South Sudan. Paperwork mattered less than who you knew, and survival depended on whether someone remembered you existed.

Three hours in, without warning, she lunged.

She screamed something I didn't understand, swinging wildly. One hand connected with my cheekbone—a sharp crack that sent heat spreading across my face. The other tangled in my hair and yanked hard. My scalp burned. My head snapped back against the wall, skull meeting concrete with a dull thud that rang through my teeth.

I thought, *Don't touch her.*

Then I thought, *That rule no longer applies.*

I pulled back and drove a fist into her abdomen. Not hard—just enough. The impact traveled up my forearm, soft flesh giving way. She folded with a grunt, air rushing out of her. It didn't slow her. She came again.

The door burst open. Heavy boots on concrete. A guard rushed in and punched her square in the jaw. The sound was wet and final. She dropped instantly, dead weight hitting the floor. He dragged her unconscious body out like a sack of grain, her heels scraping the concrete.

He turned to me, eyes narrowed.

"You call yourself a man? Next time, act like one."

The door slammed shut. The echo hung in the air.

I sat there in the silence, heart hammering against my ribs. My face throbbed where she'd connected, already swelling. The back of my head pulsed. I checked my ribs—sore but nothing broken. My hands were shaking. I pressed them against the concrete floor, cold and gritty, trying to steady them.

Less than twenty-four hours in the country, and I was already in a jail cell with a murderer.

I laughed. Couldn't help it. A short, sharp sound that bounced off the walls. The absurdity of it was almost funny. Almost.

I'd come to South Sudan to help. To document. To do something that mattered. And here I was—sitting on the floor of a holding cell, tasting copper, having just punched a woman high on heroin who may or may not have actually killed her husband.

I had no phone. No way to contact anyone.

The guard's words kept replaying: *"You call yourself a man? Next time, act like one."*

I wasn't sure what "next time" he was imagining. I wasn't sure I wanted to find out.

Time passed. Minutes or hours, I couldn't tell. The bulb overhead flickered occasionally. My breathing slowed. Sweat cooled on my neck. I sat against the wall, knees pulled up, waiting for something to happen.

Then footsteps echoed down the corridor.

A man appeared at the bars—older, thick around the middle, uniform pressed and fitted. He wore a half-cocked beret like he'd studied war movies and decided that's what command looked like. Not a guard. Someone with rank.

He looked in, took in the scene—the empty cell, me alone against the wall, whatever marks were visible on my face—and laughed.

"She win?"

I snorted despite myself.

***

Two days earlier, I'd been in Los Angeles shooting fashion. Models on the cyc, chewing bubble gum during takes, wearing clothes that cost more than most people made in a month. I was a software engineer who'd traded code for cameras, restless, looking for something I couldn't name. I was done with it like so many other things in life. I wanted more. I needed more.

The headlines kept flashing: South Sudan. Civil war. One hundred thousand starving.

I bought a ticket. Didn't think it through. Told myself I wanted to help, document what was happening, make a difference. But that wasn't the whole truth.

***

The small turboprop began its descent, dropping fast toward a destination I barely understood. Eighteen hours of travel had worn me down. I hated flying—always had. The confinement, the pressure, the knowledge that if something went wrong, there was nowhere to go.

The plane dropped. My stomach rose into my chest. Below us, the earth looked stripped bare. No forests. No rivers. Just cracked land and dirt tracks that led nowhere. It looked unfinished. Abandoned.

The engines whined as we descended. The airframe shuddered. I gripped the armrest, knuckles white.

The plane touched down hard, tires shrieking against cracked tarmac. My body slammed forward against the seatbelt. The runway ran out beneath us. Wrecked aircraft lined the far end—a boneyard of those who came before. Passengers erupted into applause. Survival had become routine.

I unbuckled and stood, legs unsteady.

Stepping off the plane, the heat hit like a wall. Not desert dry, not tropical humidity, but something in between. The sun was white and merciless. The air smelled like diesel and dust and something else I couldn't place. My skin, already flushed, started to sweat immediately.

An elderly man moved slowly near the plane, unloading luggage by hand. He glanced at me.

"Which ones are yours?"

I nodded toward my green Osprey bag—pristine compared to everything else, purchased days earlier with a gift card from my family.

He grabbed both bags and tossed them toward me. They hit the pavement and skidded, fabric scraping against cracked tarmac. The Osprey picked up its first scar. "You take them now; that's your job." Something in his tone made it feel less like instruction and more like test.

Then a stocky man in blue-and-black camouflage appeared. His gaze locked on me.

"Welcome to Juba." A crooked smile.

Inside the makeshift airport, nothing was straight: chipped walls, uneven floors, stale air that hadn't moved in years. A single wooden counter worn smooth by hands. Men in dark uniforms moved slowly, searching bags.

"Place your bags on the counter."

The process was mechanical. One man's attention stopped on lithium batteries tucked in my bag.

"What are these for?"

"My flashlight and camera gear." I kept my voice steady.

He paused, holding the batteries. His eyes flicked to me, then back to them. Testing.

I held his gaze. No words. No expression.

He glanced around the room—checking if anyone was watching. Then he set the batteries back and marked my bag with white chalk. An X. Clearance or reminder—I couldn't tell.

At the next counter, the young woman behind plexiglass didn't smile.

"Passport."

I slid it across. She flipped through pages fast, eyes cold and sharp.

"And your invitation letter, please."

"Invitation letter?"

"You cannot come in without one."

Before I could respond, a hulking man in camouflage stepped forward. A thick gold ring caught the light on his finger—too large, like it had belonged to someone else first. My stomach dropped.

"You don't have it. Come with me."

He led me down a narrow hallway stained with God knows what, then stopped. "First door on the left."

He outweighed me by a hundred pounds, easy. I was in a country where I had no friends, no allies, no idea what came next. The whole thing felt like a scene straight out of a spy thriller, except I wasn't Jason Bourne. No weapons. No fancy footwork. Just me.

I stepped inside.

The room was dim—a chair, a small rusted table, a flickering bulb. The door clicked shut behind me. The lock turned. Cockroaches skittered across the floor and disappeared into a crack in the corner. The place felt more like a torture room than an office.

I stood there, pulse thumping in my ears. Mouth dry.

Then he returned.

"You're being deported." He said it like he'd said it a thousand times. To him, I was just a problem to remove.

My stomach dropped. I glanced out the window. The plane that had brought me was taxiing, getting ready to leave—the last flight of the day. The engine whine grew distant.

I let out a short laugh, involuntary.

"Why are you laughing?"

"Because the only plane that can take me home is leaving."

His eyes followed the plane as it lifted. Then he smiled faintly, and let out a quiet laugh. The tension broke.

"I think you might be having a lucky day. I like you. I'm going to help you, my friend."

Minutes later, he returned with my passport and the invitation letter.

I went back to the counter. Same woman, same expression. She glanced at him, then stamped a visa across my pages.

"Welcome to Juba."

I thought I'd made it. I was wrong.

***

Less than a day later, I sat on a concrete floor in a jail cell outside the city.

No invitation letter could save you from everything.

The police chief slowly leaned in, smiling.

"You want out?" he asked, a faint grin tugging at his lips as he held my gaze.

"How much?"

3

Deadly Ground

THE CELL DOOR OPENED, and I followed the police chief to his small makeshift office. I sat in a cold metal chair; he settled behind an old, faded wooden desk. Photos were taped to the walls, each one a frozen fragment of power, violence, or authority. On his desk sat my Canon camera, complete with a telephoto lens. I was stunned it was still there—I had assumed it had already been sold somewhere in town.

He scanned the room, his eyes resting on the images. I remained silent.

"I will let you out if you do me one favor." He met my gaze with a kind grin.

"I'm listening."

"See all these photos?" His arms swept toward the walls. A proud smile gleamed across his face.

I nodded, unsure of what was coming next.

"I want more—of me and my men. Powerful photos. Print them, laminate them, hang them on my walls. Then I will let you out. And we will become friends."

Wait. Was I really hearing this? The exact thing that had gotten me into this mess was now the key to my release. Photography. The crime was now the solution. I'd been locked up for taking pictures without permission, and now the chief wanted me to take more—of him, staged and printed like campaign posters. It might have been funny if I hadn't been sitting in a cell minutes before with a woman who'd just tried to kill me.

I stood, extended my hand, and he shook it. "Deal."

I didn't come to South Sudan with a plan. I came because I saw headlines about 100,000 people starving and I had a camera and didn't know what else to do with my life. I figured I'd show up and see if there was something useful I could do.

***

Over the next few weeks, I visited aid organizations around Juba. Most of them operated out of compounds with high walls and razor wire. Inside, the staff—a mix of career humanitarians and college students earning academic credit—worked on logistics, paperwork, distributions. Outside the walls, people were dying. The contrast was hard to ignore.

***

One evening I received an invitation to dinner from a group of NGO workers I'd recently met. They were a mix of seasoned professionals and fresh-faced idealists. The dinner was served in a makeshift hall tucked behind temporary tents: rice, beans, some leathery meat, stale bread, bottled water that smelled like fluoride. It wasn't much, but what nourished me that evening wasn't the food—it was the conversation.

At first the talk was innocuous—logistics, ongoing projects, the endless paperwork that seemed to define NGO life. Then the conversation shifted. They told me about a recent intern who had joined their ranks. She'd been there just a few weeks, one of a group of eager volunteers sent to earn college credits, to do something meaningful. She was twenty-four, but already burdened with an idealistic vision of saving the world. Her enthusiasm had been infectious, her eyes bright with the energy only youth can carry. Yet her story had taken a tragic turn: she'd left the camp suddenly, diagnosed with AIDS after a relationship with a local resident—one of the many unspoken dangers in the aid community.

No one said it outright, but the room went quiet. Her intentions had been good, I was told. She'd come to help, to do something that mattered. But she'd gotten involved with someone local, crossed lines she shouldn't have crossed, and paid for it. It happens out here. The isolation gets to people. Professional boundaries blur when you're that far from home, that lonely, that convinced you're doing something important.

It wasn't uncommon, I was told, for people in her position to break down. They had a term for it—"emotional dysregulation"—which didn't come close to describing what actually happened. It wouldn't be the last time I saw someone fall apart. When you're that far from home, carrying that much idealism and no real sense of what you're walking into, the lines get blurry fast.

Some people simply couldn't handle it—the isolation, the constant reminder of what couldn't be fixed, the awareness that their efforts always seemed small against so much suffering.

I sometimes wonder what became of her. Did she find her way back? Rebuild a life? Or was she left behind, just another casualty in the machinery of aid work?

The hardest part wasn't what happened to her. It was how quickly everyone moved on. No one wanted to talk about it. The aid world has a way of protecting itself—burying stories like hers, refusing to admit what actually happens out here. I didn't know it then, but her story wasn't unique. It was common.

We tell ourselves we're protecting the next generation. We're not. We send them in just as blind as we were. The interns keep coming—young, eager, convinced they can help. Some make it. Some don't. The ones who break aren't talked about. They just disappear, and we replace them with the next batch.

***

The work had other dangers too. Physical ones.

I spent time with a mine-clearance team in South Sudan. The civil war had been over for years, but the mines were still there—buried in fields, under roads, places where kids walked to school. The team's job was to find them and detonate them before someone stepped on one. Nobody paid much attention to this work. It was slow, technical, and you could die doing it.

The task before the mine-clearance team was monumental. Limited resources, little public awareness, uneven coordination among factions meant progress was slow and setbacks common. Yet the mine clearers—a diverse group who had chosen to risk their lives for the sake of others—refused to surrender to the scale of their mission. Their work came down to inches, a painstaking process where a single misstep could end a life.

I was given the chance to witness—and even assist with—the work of the mine-clearance team, watching as they moved across terrain with a combination of technology and human instinct.

Their first tool was the Mine Wolf—a hulking machine with rotating chains that beat the ground violently, triggering mines to detonate beneath it. The machine was built to survive the blasts, clearing paths by forcing the explosions on its terms. Once it finished a section, the next phase began.

Next, a bomb technician stepped forward, wearing a heavy Kevlar-and-Nomex suit and carrying a metal detector. Every step mattered. The earth beneath him could erupt without warning. When he located a mine—in this case a German S-mine, commonly called a Bouncing Betty—he marked the spot, knelt, and carefully dug around it until the device was fully exposed. Only then would he place a small explosive charge beside it, retreat, and trigger a controlled blast that detonated the mine through sympathetic detonation.

In the final stage, a dog—its nose trained to detect the subtle traces that machines and humans might miss—entered. The dog was the ultimate line of defense. Its stillness, when it sat motionless, signaled the presence of a hidden threat that had eluded all others. The process was slow and deliberate, and the fact that it worked at all was a testament to the team's perseverance. But when the land was finally cleared—when the last mine had been neutralized—the transformation was striking.

The land, once cleared, became usable again. Families planted crops where mines had been. It wasn't much, but in a country like this, any safe ground mattered.

Not everyone was honest about where the mines were. Some people reported false minefields—claiming land was contaminated when it wasn't—because they knew the clearance teams would till the soil with the Mine Wolf. Free plowing. It wasn't right, but given the desperation, it was hard to blame them.

On one occasion we were clearing ground near a primary school—just north of the property line. The area was vast, far too large for the children to walk around, so each morning they gathered at one edge of the minefield and waited.

I watched them meet in small clusters, laughing, playing, hugging one another as if this were any ordinary schoolyard. Then, in an instant, they would break into a full sprint across the mine-contaminated field, racing toward the other side and on to class. In the afternoon the same scene played out in reverse—children collecting themselves at the edge, sharing quick embraces, then darting back across the deadly ground as though danger were nothing more than a shadow.

Watching them was almost unbearable.

Not because they were reckless. They weren't. They were simply children born into a world where survival had become routine, where running across a minefield was as normal as crossing a street. Back home, children worry about homework, friendships, what's for dinner. Here, they worried about stepping wrong. And they accepted it. That was the part that cut deepest—the acceptance. The way they laughed and played right up until the moment they had to run, then sprinted without hesitation, without complaint, as if this was just how life worked.

Their laughter carried across the field, bright and unguarded, a sound that should have belonged to a playground anywhere else in the world. But here it was layered over deadly ground, and that contrast—innocence against inevitability—made the silent threat of the mines feel monstrous.

I thought about my own childhood. The worst danger I faced was a scraped knee, maybe a fall from a tree. These kids faced death twice a day just to go to school. And they didn't know any different. That was their normal. This was the world they inherited, and they navigated it with a courage I'm not sure I could have managed at their age.

We cleared that field as fast as we could. Not fast enough.

***

As time stretched on in Juba, some lessons were not taught—they were experienced.

One such lesson came as an unspoken rule: never cross the bridge over the Nile after dusk.

I didn't know it was a rule. It wasn't in any guidebook. No local driver or official had mentioned it. Just like I hadn't known I needed an invitation letter to enter the country. Just like I hadn't known taking photos required paperwork. South Sudan had rules—plenty of them—but nobody told you what they were. You learned by breaking them. And if you were lucky, you survived the lesson. This was one more I would have to learn firsthand.

It began innocuously enough. We were invited to join colleagues for dinner at a Chinese restaurant in Juba City. The food was extraordinary in the way only a meal away from home can be: rich, complex flavors that felt like a small luxury.

As the evening wore on and the last plates were cleared, soft conversation settled into the stillness of night. Time had slipped away. The sun had vanished behind the horizon.

Then, abruptly, someone leaned over. "You shouldn't cross the bridge after dark. Too many hold-ups, and the patrols don't have patience for outsiders."

The warning came suddenly, too late. After sunset the bridge became a flashpoint—guards jittery, checkpoints unpredictable, the risk of confrontation high. And most of the guards were kids on drugs.

We rushed to the vehicle, panic quietly mounting, hoping to cross before darkness swallowed the landscape. But as we approached, it became clear we wouldn't make it. The bridge—our only path—lay ahead, illuminated only by the faint glow of headlights.

The checkpoint stood ahead, a single barrier between us and the camp on the other side. The guards—young men barely out of their teens—stood watching as the vehicle approached.

We slowed to a stop. I could see their faces now in the headlights—sunken, twitchy, wrong. One of them stepped forward, rifle already raised. Before I could process what was happening, the cold barrel of an AK-47 pressed against the side of my head, the force making my ears ring.

The young soldier—no more than eighteen—had blood-shot eyes, unfocused. His hands trembled slightly, but his body was unnaturally still, like he was holding himself together by force of will.

His voice was rough, thick with something between anger and confusion. "Why are you crossing the bridge? Are you a spy?"

I responded carefully. "No. We just had dinner. We lost track of time. Our camp is just on the other side. I apologize."

His eyes darted left, then right, scanning the shadows. He didn't seem convinced. Then a soft nudge at my side. A friend seated next to me pressed something into my lap: a six-pack of local Tusker beer.

I glanced at my friend, steady and unflinching, before returning my gaze to the soldier. The kid saw the beer. His expression shifted—not much, but enough.

"Give it to me."

I didn't hesitate. I reached down, grabbed the beer, handed it over. He took it without another word. Everything shifted. The gun pressed against my temple was lowered. His posture relaxed, shoulders slumping as if some weight had been lifted.

"Move along."

That was it. No other words. No questions. The tension dissolved as suddenly as it had appeared.

There's a story that drifts through Juba, one of those whispers that harden into fact with each retelling. They say there used to be two bridges spanning the Nile, but one night one was blown to pieces—sabotaged, according to the locals. Since then, only a single bridge remains, guarded like a lifeline. To cross after dark is to mark yourself as a suspect.

We drove on in silence. The bridge receded into the rearview mirror, but it wasn't the bridge that lingered in my mind—it was the soldier. The way he'd stood there, his stiff posture softening at the simple arrival of beer. In that fleeting moment I saw the contrast between the uniform and the person beneath it, the fragile humanity that often gets stripped away in places like this.

We were lucky. Perhaps too lucky. But that's Juba: a place where the rules of survival aren't written, only whispered.

4

The Lie

THAT UNEASY BALANCE BETWEEN survival and exploitation stayed with me as my time in South Sudan neared its end. Yet even as I prepared to leave, another invitation arrived—one I couldn't refuse: a visit to a children's hospital in the center of town arranged by a woman from a pediatric NGO.

I'd already seen the toll war had taken on the land, but inside the crumbling walls of the hospital, I felt it on the most vulnerable: the children. The building was nothing like the sanitized images NGOs often show. No gleaming floors, no bright walls, no sense of hope at first glance—only decay. Paint peeled in long strips, dust coated every surface, and the air smelled of antiseptic mixed with neglect. Piles of refuse—discarded syringes, soiled sheets, broken equipment—crowded the corners. The hospital had been built years earlier by a UN program, but whoever built it had never come back. No equipment. No staff. Just walls.

The stark reality hit hardest when I saw who was left to navigate these empty shells. Mothers sat in silence, cradling sick children, their faces drawn by exhaustion. Their eyes carried hopelessness, each glance an acknowledgment that survival was uncertain. Doctors were scarce, and those who remained were stretched impossibly thin, shuttling between beds with a frantic precision that still couldn't meet the needs before them.

Every sound—the cough of a child, the scrape of a chair, the soft whine of machinery struggling to work—carried through the ward. This hospital, one of the few still standing in the area, had become a monument to systemic failure.

Most aid organizations had long since withdrawn, retreating to "safer" areas. Our last stop was a room for children who weren't going to make it. Mothers sat silently, clutching their children, listening to labored breathing, soft moans, whispered prayers. Waiting for the end.

There were no doctors here, not in this ward. No interventions, no treatments, nothing but the hard truth of who could not be saved. The room pulsed with the immediacy of loss, a place where helplessness was felt from every side.

It was unbearable to watch. Children dying from diseases that had been curable for decades—treatable, preventable, solved in every wealthy country. But not here. The medications existed. They sat in warehouses, in pharmacies, in hospitals thousands of miles away. They just never made it to South Sudan.

Each shallow breath was a failure. Not the mothers' failure—they were doing everything they could. It was everyone else's. The bureaucrats who delayed shipments. The aid organizations that pulled out when things got dangerous. The world that had decided some children were worth saving and others weren't.

The mothers stayed. They whispered prayers, traced their children's faces, held on when there was nothing left to hold onto. I watched them and realized I was witnessing something no statistic could measure: what it looks like when love refuses to let go, even when everything else already has.

***

On my last morning, I visited one of the IDP (Internally Displaced People) camps on the outskirts of Juba. Thousands lived there—families who'd fled violence, waiting for safety that would probably never come. I walked through the camp with a local guide, handing out what little we had, listening.

A man started following me. Not close—always about ten paces back, eyes on the ground. When I turned to look at him, he'd stop, head down, wouldn't meet my eyes. This went on for half an hour.

Finally, I asked the guide. "Why is he following me?"

The guide walked back to him. They spoke quietly. The man's voice rose—desperate, pleading. The guide nodded and came back.

"He wants you to help find his family."

"Where are they?"

"He doesn't know. They got separated five years ago. They were running—people were hunting them. They agreed to meet here if they got split up. He's been waiting ever since."

I looked back at the man. He stood there, still, watching me. Waiting for me to say something that would help. Waiting for me to fix it.

"Five years?" I said.

"Yes."

"And his family?"

The guide's face changed. Something heavy settled there. He looked at the man, then back at me. Lowered his voice.

"They're dead. The people hunting them—they caught them. Everyone here knows. But no one's told him."

The words didn't land right at first. I had to process them.

"Everyone knows?"

"Yes."

"And no one's told him?"

The guide looked at me like I was missing something obvious.

"What would it change? Right now he has hope. He wakes up every morning with a reason. You want to take that from him?"

I stood there trying to find an answer. There wasn't one.

The man was still watching me. Still waiting. Still believing I could help.

I had nothing for him. No way to find people who'd been dead for five years. Just the truth—and the truth would destroy the only thing keeping him alive.

So I did nothing.

I nodded at him—tried to make it look sympathetic, like I understood, like I cared—and I walked away. I left him standing there in the same spot where he'd stood every morning for five years, waiting for people who were never coming back.

I didn't tell him. No one did.

And he's probably still there. Still waiting. Still hoping. Still waking up every morning with a reason to keep breathing, built on a lie everyone around him agreed to protect.

I think about him sometimes. Wonder if he ever found out. Wonder if it would have been kinder to tell him. Wonder if the guide was right—that hope, even false hope, is better than nothing.

I don't know. I still don't know.

That night, alone in my quarters, I let myself think about what I'd seen. Not grief—grief is a luxury in this work. You don't unpack it. You just carry it forward. But I thought about the children in the hospital. The mothers who wouldn't let go. The man still waiting at the camp. And all the others I'd never meet—the ones already lost, the ones who'd never know safety or health or even a bare chance at living.

South Sudan had taught me something I hadn't expected: that sometimes the cruelest thing isn't violence or death, but hope built on a foundation that no longer exists. And sometimes, the kindest thing you can do is walk away and let someone keep believing, even when you know the truth.

I left Juba that evening.

The man, I imagine, is still waiting.

***

Sitting on the plane out, I kept thinking about why I'd come to South Sudan in the first place.

If I'm being honest, there was another reason I chose places like this.

I was tired. Not the kind of tired that sleep fixes, but the kind that makes you wonder if waking up is worth the effort. I was a Christian, and that closed certain doors—I couldn't end my life deliberately. But I could put myself in situations where death might find me honorably. High-risk humanitarian work in the most dangerous places on earth seemed like a solution. If I died doing something that mattered, no one would call it suicide. They'd call it sacrifice.

The problem was, I kept surviving.

Every mission I walked away from. Every close call that should have been the end—wasn't. The jail cell, the gun to my head at the checkpoint, the children running through mine-fields, the hospital ward where hope went to die—I witnessed all of it and kept breathing.

I didn't know yet that this work wasn't going to kill me. It was going to teach me how to live.

5

Half There

COMING BACK HAS NEVER felt like returning home. The streets were the same, the people the same, the air carried the same smell—but something inside me had shifted. I moved through familiar places like a visitor. My body was here, but my mind remained half a world away, on a dirt airstrip, listening for the cry of someone in need.

Days passed in a dull drift. I tried to rejoin normal life—coffee shops, grocery stores, small talk—but it all felt insubstantial, like the world I returned to had lost its gleam. At night I lay awake, replaying moments that refused to leave: faces, noise, sudden silences.

The job I'd tolerated now felt meaningless. The future I'd imagined no longer fit. I stood in my own life like a spectator, aware that something was off but unsure how to belong again.

I kept thinking about the people back in South Sudan. The man waiting in the dust. The kids darting through minefields. The mothers in the hospital ward. And I kept asking myself:

what the hell are we doing here? All of us, in our comfortable lives, worrying about jobs and bills, about what people think—while people are dying from problems we solved decades ago. When did human beings start to lose their significance? How could I not ask myself that?

It wasn't anger exactly. It was clarity—a kind of seeing-through-things I hadn't before. In *Untamed*, Glennon Doyle writes: *"Because once we feel, know, and dare to imagine more for ourselves, we cannot unfeel, unknow, or unimagine. There is no going back."* I had become a believer. Polite conversations felt hollow. The concerns people had—traffic, promotions, social media—felt small. Not because they didn't matter to them, but because I'd seen what actually mattered, and this wasn't it.

I tried explaining it to Sarah over coffee.

"There were kids running through minefields just to get to school," I said.

She nodded, glanced at her phone. "That's heavy. Hey, did you see the Warriors game last night?"

I stopped talking. She hadn't heard a word.

I found out years later there was a name for it. The way rooms full of people felt like static. The way I could read a minefield better than I could read a dinner conversation. Asperger's. It didn't explain everything. But it explained enough.

What I didn't expect was how much I learned about myself out there. I'd always thought of myself as someone who avoided confrontation, who preferred the sidelines. South Sudan proved me wrong. When a situation demanded action, I acted. When people needed help, I helped. I didn't freeze. I didn't run. And the patience—the long, grinding patience—surprised me too. Waiting in that jail cell. Watching the bomb tech dig around a mine for an hour. Standing helpless while the waiting man begged for his family. I'd always been restless, impatient, but out there, patience wasn't optional—it was survival. In silence—as I had learned—many questions could be answered, and in silence, many answers could be spoken. It was in those quiet, tense moments that the questions I'd wrestled with as a teenager came alive: Why do some rise while others fall? What makes a life matter? Why do some act like they're untouchable, above everyone else? Why do some have more than anyone else could need? And why does the wrong way almost always pay the most? We scream about injustice—but every day, the easier road is still the one paved with cruelty and greed. Those questions were no longer abstract. They clawed at me. They burned through my sleep, my skin, my bones. I couldn't ignore them. I had seen what actually mattered, and the world I'd once worried about—traffic, promotions, social media—felt small, hollow, insignificant.

My mom called the week I got back.

"So when are you looking for a real job?"

"I'm working on something. Humanitarian—"

"That's not a job, Burke. That's a hobby. You have a degree. Use it."

The line went quiet. I didn't have an answer she'd accept.

I began scribbling in notebooks—half-formed sketches of a world where help could arrive without pretense, without slideshows or charity dinners. I called a few people who might understand—those who had glimpsed the edge with me and hadn't flinched. Some laughed. Some didn't answer. A few—just a handful—listened.

I started researching organizations, making lists of problems I could address, testing the edges of what I was willing to endure. Humanitarian work was vast: rescue, logistics, medical, building, coordination, advocacy, food. Each path seemed critical, but which could I pursue without experience or credentials?

Most people find a role in an established organization, learn the ropes, and carve a niche. I had skipped the line. No safety net, no mentor, no infrastructure. In all honesty, I was starting at the end, not the beginning—plunging straight into the chaos of need, hoping my instincts would be enough.

Some nights I stared at the ceiling, wondering if I had made a colossal mistake. How could I claim to help anyone when I couldn't define "help" in my own terms? The scale of need made my head spin. But beneath the anxiety, something stirred. A stubborn refusal to wait for permission. A visceral understanding that hesitation can cost lives.

I didn't have a roadmap or prior experience—but I had perspective, awareness, and the refusal to look away.

I started connecting threads. Every conversation, every minor insight, slowly illuminated the edges of what could become actionable. Some nights, after long calls or scribbling until the ink blurred, I felt small victories—an idea landing, a conversation taking shape, a step forward.

Slowly, the fog began to lift. I wasn't clear on what form my work would take, but I had discovered something: forward motion, no matter how tentative, was the only way to form clarity from chaos. Each small step tethered me to a part of me I thought I'd lost—courage, patience, stubbornness, the instinct to act even when exhausted.

I sat back in the dark one night, the hum of the city faint through the blinds. My thoughts wandered to the next steps, to the faces I'd carried home, to the work I didn't yet understand but was beginning to shape. The pull returned—a quiet, insistent tug.

Somewhere between counting shadows and wondering if sleep would ever return, my phone rang. Not a polite ring. A shrill, middle-of-the-night demand that jerked me fully awake.

I cracked one eye open, squinting at the sliver of light bleeding through the blinds. Still dark. Either way too late or way too early—the hour when bad news traveled fastest. I groped for my phone, bracing for whatever awaited on the other end.

The name on the screen: Corey. One of the few people who could call at this hour without landing in voicemail. We had history. Long nights, bad ideas, situations demanding an exit strategy. Geography didn't matter—he'd always show up, no questions asked, when things went sideways.

I answered.

6

The Eye

OREY DIDN'T WASTE A syllable. "Get dressed. Now. Meet me at the diner."

That was all I needed.

I threw on clothes, heart already thrumming with that sharp adrenaline—the kind that remembers sudden scrambles and the cost of hesitation. My bag was half-packed, either from habit or some deeper instinct, as if part of me had known this moment was coming.

Almost six months had passed since South Sudan, though it felt less like time and more like a long limbo. Every day I found myself drifting back to the same place—the gym. It wasn't routine. It was ritual. The clatter of weights, the rhythm of breath, the burn in my muscles—it was the only language my body still understood. It grounded me when the rest of life felt unmoored.

I showed up before sunrise, moving through reps with a focus bordering on obsession. Not chasing strength—it was clarity I sought. The rare moments when my mind would stop looping images from the field.

Between sets, I scrolled through humanitarian organizations, scanning missions, failures, bureaucratic traps. None fit. Too slow. Too polished. Too safe. Boardrooms and committees weren't for me. I wanted dirt, immediacy, places where need was raw and the cost real.

But I also knew I was missing something. South Sudan had stripped me down, exposed instincts I didn't know I had—but it also showed me the limits of just acting on instinct. I needed to understand what drove me. Why I couldn't sit still. Why comfort felt like suffocation.

So I started reading. Not for credentials or theory—for myself. Jonathan Livingston Seagull, Ishmael, The Monk Who Sold His Ferrari, The Power of Now. Every book by Carlos Castaneda, everything Allan Watts wrote. I dove into human behavior, religion, spirituality—anything that could help me see what I was becoming.

I wasn't looking for answers in those books. I was looking for a framework—something to make sense of the pull I felt, the restlessness that wouldn't let go. Jung talked about the call—the moment you hear it, you either respond or stay asleep. Most people bury it under routine, comfort, distraction. I couldn't anymore. I'd walked in places where life and death breathed side by side. The call wasn't theoretical anymore—it was alive. Every heartbeat, every step, every decision demanded a response. I felt it pressing into my chest, the burden of each choice stretching into the lives I touched. Knowledge alone could no longer explain it. I had to live it, answer it, or risk walking through the world half-awake, deaf to the pull that claimed everything.

The books didn't change me. They just gave me language for what was already happening.

And always, beneath it all, that pull—like a hand on your shoulder you couldn't shake. Something unfinished. Something calling. Purpose didn't announce itself. It came as a gnawing tug you couldn't name, a question that wouldn't stop echoing. You chased it, or it dragged you forward.

By the time I hit the street, the city was still asleep. But I no longer moved through it as a spectator. Every sense was alert. Every lesson from the field, every failure and misstep, every sharp memory was standing by. The night wasn't just darkness—it was the threshold of something new.

The diner's red OPEN 24 Hours sign buzzed above the door. Inside, it smelled like burnt coffee. Corey was already in a booth at the back, hunched over his phone, eyes locked on something he couldn't look away from.

He glanced up when I slid into the seat. "Couldn't sleep. Not after seeing this."

He turned the phone toward me.

Footage filled the display—overhead shot, shaky, likely from a news chopper. The storm sprawled across the horizon, dark and swollen, rotating in a way that didn't look natural. A lowering base dipped toward the earth, debris beginning to flicker at the edges. Sirens bled faintly through the audio. The crawl at the bottom read: **Tornado Emergency**.

My stomach tightened. "You've been watching this all night?"

"Since it started building," he said, eyes fixed on the screen. "This was just before it dropped."

He scrubbed a hand through his hair. "They knew it was coming. Said it could touch down any minute. Whole town sitting in the path—power flickering, comms already getting spotty."

It wasn't just this feed. Clips were everywhere—storm chasers parked on backroads, phones shaking in their hands, live streams cutting in and out as the sky twisted above them. Social media was flooded with it. Everyone watching the same storm, the same rotation, the same moment building toward something no one could stop.

I watched the screen, the slow, deliberate rotation tightening. Knowing what came next didn't make it easier to look at.

Corey leaned back, eyes rimmed red. "I couldn't just sit around... and I figured you wouldn't either."

Corey wasn't just a friend. He was one of the few people who understood why I couldn't stay still. We'd met years earlier when my life looked nothing like this. I'd been deep in undercover work—operations where saying the wrong thing could get you killed. Corey had been a source I could trust completely. Sharp. Fearless. Built for danger. Most people talk big. Corey lived big.

He knew I was still wrestling with what my nonprofit was actually going to do. His take on it was simple: "You'll see it when it finds you."

We had the same problem. We couldn't stay home when the world was on fire.

The pull wasn't hypothetical anymore—it was immediate, visible, screaming for action.

"That's our next stop," he whispered. "We get there, we figure it out. Together."

The diner hummed with late-night chatter and clinking dishes, oblivious to the storm that had already ripped through thousands of lives. At our booth, uncertainty hovered. The plan—if you could call it that—was already taking shape. Not foolproof. Not fully articulated. But alive. And I knew: whatever I'd been searching for, this was it—the point where waiting ended, and doing began.

On the way home, I pulled out my phone and called someone I'd hoped I'd never need to call in the middle of the night: Becca.

She answered on the second ring, groggy but instantly alert. "You okay?"

"Yeah. It's not me. It's Oklahoma."

Becca was a stay-at-home mom in name only. She was a world traveler now confined to domestic life—restless, sharp, always searching for ways to turn compassion into action. Field operations were out of reach; kids and responsibilities kept her grounded. But she had airline miles in absurd abundance and a readiness to deploy them at the first hint of need. When it came to logistics, she had a gift.

I told her everything—the rotation, the warnings, the town sitting directly in its path. She didn't hesitate.

"Send me names. Full names, birthdates. Give me thirty minutes. Flights will be booked. Text them over."

Her first operation, and she sounded like she'd been running them for decades.

I paced my home while she worked—half packing, half thinking, half wondering what I was walking into again. By the time my bag was zipped, she'd texted confirmation codes, gate numbers, and a list of local contacts pulled from a network I didn't even know existed.

Becca: "You good?"

Me: "As good as I'm gonna be."

Becca: "Then go. I'm with you from here."

***

A few hours later, Corey and I converged at the airport, bags in hand, looking like we'd just crawled out of the backwoods. Heavy-duty field pants, rugged boots, dry-fit shirts meant for sweating and bleeding in, Garmin watches synced to share locations.

No words were necessary at the gate. The nod was enough.

"Ready?" Corey asked.

I adjusted my pack. "Let's go help some people."

On the plane, we went over what little we knew—and even less of what we could predict. The airport we were flying into was twenty minutes from where the storm was expected to hit—close enough to feel it if it dropped, close enough that every choice would matter immediately.

"What's the plan when we land?" Corey asked, flipping through satellite images.

"Get in. Stay ahead of it if we can. Find the people who won't get out in time."

He gave a small smile and nodded.

We weren't pretending we had a detailed mission. No one walks into a Category 5 with a tidy checklist. Purpose revealed itself only after you committed—truly committed—to stepping inside the wreckage.

The plane shuddered, and my stomach tightened—flying never got easier. You can't negotiate with the sky. You just sit there, suspended in a metal tube, trusting physics, the pilots, and prayer in equal measure. Flying was the toll you paid for this kind of work.

As the plane leveled out, I messaged Becca again.

Me: Any local contacts near the airport? Anyone willing to ride us in?

Becca: Maybe. A woman from a nearby church. She's on the fence.

I didn't blame her. While an entire state was evacuating, we were asking someone to turn around and walk straight into the disaster zone with two strangers who looked like they lived out of rucksacks.

Me: Understood. Just let her know we could use the help. Fingers crossed.

Becca: I already did. She'll decide before you land.

The cabin dimmed as the plane settled into its long stretch. Five hours isn't long in ordinary life—but here it felt like waiting backstage for a show you'd never rehearsed for. I gripped the armrest, forcing my breath steady. I ran through scenarios: power outages, roads blocked, water displacement, missing people, destroyed homes. Anything to keep my thoughts off the sky, off the plane, off the fact that we were hurtling toward uncertainty with no safety net.

Corey closed his eyes, arms crossed, but I knew he wasn't sleeping.

"You nervous?" I asked.

His eyes stayed closed. "Only about the parts I can't see."

Fair enough. That made two of us.

Outside the window, the world below drifted by—calm, unaware of the devastation waiting ahead. The contrast was jarring: serenity above, chaos below, me caught in the air between the two.

The hours passed in that strange suspended state that comes with flying—half awake, half somewhere else. I dozed in fits, never deeply. Corey did the same. The plane moved on, steady and monotonous, carrying us closer.

Then, finally, the descent began.

I could tell we were getting close long before the pilot said a word. The air changed. The smooth hum of the cabin shifted into a low, uneven growl. Tremors started under the seat, subtle at first, then steady and unrelenting. Fear has a way of announcing itself without words.

The intercom crackled. "Ladies and gentlemen, please fasten your seatbelts. We're hitting some rough air. Weather's bad but not worsening. We'll be landing shortly."

Pilots always make bad sound casual. But outside, the sky had teeth.

As we descended through heavy black clouds, the plane lurched sideways hard enough to rattle the overhead bins. I braced against the seat in front of me.

"You good?"

"Define good," I muttered, knuckles white around the arm-rest.

Another drop—sharp, sudden. Every instinct screamed to be anywhere but trapped in a shaking metal shell miles above the ground. The cabin lights flickered as the plane pitched again, drawing a gasp from behind us. I shut my eyes for a second, steadying my breath.

Then came the last drop, the worst one, like the plane had stepped off an invisible ledge.

"E-ticket ride," Corey muttered with a half-grin.

I didn't return it.

The wheels hit the runway with a violent slam, skidding, bouncing once before the brakes caught. It wasn't graceful. But it was real—solid ground beneath us again.

For a moment, I let my heart catch up to my body.

Moments like this never let you slip in unnoticed. The places that need you most greet you with turbulence, as if testing your resolve at the threshold.

Clutching our bags, we filed out behind the handful of passengers who'd braved the flight. Inside the terminal, peo-ple moved fast—too fast for an airport at this hour. A siren blared overhead. An automated voice followed, warning of worsening conditions and directing travelers to seek shelter immediately.

Airport staff were funneling crowds toward a stairwell leading down. An underground shelter. Never a good sign.

We stopped a young guard with the wide-eyed look of someone already stretched thin.

"What's going on?" I asked.

"Tornado heading this way. Forty-five minutes, maybe less. Shelter's down that hall." He pointed, already half-turned to push another family along.

"We're not backing down. We're heading in, whatever it brings, to help those who might need us."

That made him look at us. Really look.

"You're not from around here, are you?"

"No. We're here for relief work."

He studied us for a second—the boots, the packs, the way we stood. Then he nodded.

"Up the stairs. Straight ahead. God bless you both."

Then he disappeared back into the chaos, guiding everyone else underground while we headed the opposite way—toward the storm.

***

Outside, we dropped onto a concrete bench that could have been ripped from the Cold War. We were the only ones above ground. The air was heavy and warm. The sky above us was black.

We sat there in silence, watching the empty road. No cars. No movement. Just the sound of wind and distant sirens. I checked my phone—no signal. Corey did the same. Nothing to do but wait and hope Becca's contact actually showed up.

After what felt like fifteen minutes, headlights cut through the darkness. An SUV slowed and came to an abrupt stop. A woman jumped out—fit, confident, clearly in charge. She wore field pants, a T-shirt, and a trucker cap that read NOT TODAY. She leaned against the hood and smiled.

"I'm Jane, and it's pretty obvious you're the two I'm here to meet. No one else would be out here right now, that's for sure."

Corey and I exchanged a glance. We'd both expected someone more reserved—a delicate, churchgoing volunteer. Jane wasn't that. She had energy, presence, and the kind of build that said she could carry more than groceries. Great job, Becca.

We tossed our bags into the SUV. I took the passenger seat, Corey climbed in back, and Jane hit the gas. After a few turns, the highway opened ahead—empty and black.

"The attendant said there was another tornado coming," I said. "Any truth to that?"

Jane didn't answer right away. Her eyes flicked to the rearview mirror, then back to the road. A few moments passed in silence.

Then: "There it is."

I followed her gaze to the rearview mirror. Behind us, another tornado was already moving across the sky—a black-and-gray wall of clouds, massive, heading straight for us.

The rain hit. Hard. Sheets of water hammering the windshield. The wind picked up fast and fierce. Jane reached for the radio. Static crackled, then a voice cut through:

"Warning: Confirmed Category 5 tornado in Moore, Oklahoma. All residents seek immediate shelter."

Corey and I locked eyes. His concern mirrored my own.

The words hit me like a punch. My stomach lurched. My mind—normally fast, calculating—froze.

Jane stayed focused. Calm. Controlled. But the truth was clear: there was no turning back now.

"We need to find shelter—fast. This one isn't just big. It's a monster." Jane's voice cut through the chaos, sharp and urgent.

She glanced at me, eyes filled with a question I didn't have an answer for. What do you do when something coming for you doesn't care if you survive?

Then—a sliver of hope. Vehicles huddled beneath an overpass. An ambulance and firetruck tucked in with them, engines quiet.

"We join them. Find cover. Wait it out."

Jane didn't hesitate. Foot slammed on the gas. The engine roared as we barreled toward the overpass. Inch by inch, we closed in on the massive concrete pillars—the last barrier between us and the storm.

When we were underneath it, she killed the engine. Everything went quiet except for the distant roar of wind.

Faces around us were pale, hands gripping steering wheels like lifelines. Vehicles huddled. Waiting. Praying.

The tornado came. Wind tore through trees, snapping trunks like dry twigs. Debris spun through the air—branches, roof shingles, chunks of metal. Rain hammered sideways. The sound was massive, like a freight train bearing down on us. The car shook. Jane hunched over the steering wheel, gripping it tight. The roar was constant, relentless.

Highway signs bent under the wind, metal screaming as bolts gave way. One tore completely free and tumbled across the road like a playing card. Branches the size of telephone poles flew past. A roof shingle slammed into the concrete pillar next to us with a crack that made me flinch. Then another. Then a steady barrage of debris—wood, metal, pieces of buildings I couldn't identify—all of it rattling against the guardrails, hammering the overpass.

Rain didn't fall. It drove sideways in solid sheets, so thick I couldn't see more than a few feet beyond the windshield. The trees on either side of the highway bent almost horizontal, their trunks whipping back and forth like they were trying to rip themselves out of the ground.

The tornado didn't just destroy things. It chose them. A tree would stand untouched while the one next to it exploded into splinters. An abandoned car twenty yards away lifted off the ground and flipped—once, twice—before slamming back down on its roof. I watched a stop sign bend, twist, then snap clean off, the pole spinning end over end into the black.

The sky looked wrong. Not just dark—green and gray, swirling, sick. The light had this strange quality, like dusk in the middle of a storm, everything dim and flat and unnatural.

Inside the car, the noise made it hard to think. Not just loud—overwhelming. The roar pressed against my chest, vibrated through the seat, filled my ears until I couldn't hear anything else. Jane's knuckles were white on the steering wheel. Corey hadn't moved. Neither had I. We just sat there, waiting, watching the tornado tear through everything in reach.

And there was nothing we could do but sit there and hope our position held.

And then—nothing.

A pause.

Silence so sudden, so absolute, it felt unnatural. Like the air itself had been ripped from the world.

The eye.

7

Emptied Pockets

S OMEHOW, IMPOSSIBLY, WE WERE inside it—a place most people never imagine occupying, not because it's unreachable, but because instinct tells you to stay away. And yet there we were, suspended in the heart of something biblical.

The silence hit first. Not quiet—silence. Absolute. The kind that makes your ears ring because they're searching for sound that isn't there. The roar of wind, rain, debris—all of it just stopped. Cut off like someone had flipped a switch.

My breathing was the loudest thing I could hear. Each inhale, each exhale. The sound of my own heartbeat pulsing in my ears. Jane's hand gripping the steering wheel so tight the leather creaked.

The air felt different. Thick. Heavy. Like I was at the bottom of an ocean with weights holding me down. My ears popped—once, twice—the pressure change sudden and violent. My skin prickled. Every hair on my arms stood up. Static electricity, maybe, or something else I didn't understand.

I rolled down the window without thinking. Needed to feel it, to prove this was real. The air that came in wasn't hot or cold—it was nothing. Neutral. Wrong in a way I couldn't articulate. It didn't smell like rain or earth or ozone. It smelled like nothing. Like the air itself had been stolen from the moment.

Outside, the world had transformed. Debris hung suspended in the still air—leaves, pieces of paper, small branches—floating lazily like they'd forgotten which way was down. Some drifted slowly to the ground. Others just hovered. Physics operating on different rules.

I couldn't stop staring. Part of me knew I should look away, focus on something else, but I couldn't. The wrongness was mesmerizing—beautiful and terrifying at the same time. The kind of thing that makes you understand why people freeze when they should run.

Corey leaned forward between the seats, eyes tracking something in the distance. I heard him exhale, low and quiet. Not quite a whistle, not quite a breath. Just sound.

"You seeing this?" he muttered.

"Yeah," I said. My voice sounded flat. Absorbed by the dead air.

Jane didn't say anything. Her eyes were locked on the rearview mirror, tracking the wall of black behind us. The tornado. Still there. Circling. Waiting.

We were in its center. In the place where the storm paused to gather strength before tearing forward again.

Then it vanished. The wind roared back with renewed fury, punching through the stillness, rattling the vehicle. Objects obeyed no law but chaos: telephone poles snapped, debris skidded across asphalt, glass sprayed in a fine mist that caught the headlights before vanishing into darkness. Even the road seemed alive, bucking beneath us.

The sound was different now. Not just wind—something deeper. A low, grinding roar that vibrated through the metal of the car, through the concrete beneath us, through my bones. The kind of sound you feel more than hear.

And then the water came. Not rain—a wall of it, like someone had opened a dam overhead. It didn't fall gradually. It arrived all at once, swallowing everything in its path. The tornado was now hurling every drop of water it had gathered, and the volume was staggering.

Within seconds, the far side of the interstate was under water. Not road anymore—just brown water, deep and fast, carrying debris with it. Trees. Car parts. Chunks of buildings. All of it swept away in the current.

The road in front of us dropped off sharply. If it hadn't, we'd have been in that water too.

I stared at what now looked like a raging torrent, trying to process what I was seeing. The sheer volume of water. The speed. The way it had transformed a highway into a river in less than a minute. And then I saw movement in the current—something tumbling, spinning.

A van. Small, maybe a minivan. Caught in the surge, spinning wildly, slamming against the concrete barriers again and again. The current just tossed it around like it weighed nothing. Completely helpless.

Each impact made a hollow, metallic boom that cut through the storm. The van's side crumpled a little more with every hit. Glass shattered. Metal screamed.

We weren't the only ones watching. Everyone was—the firefighters, the ambulance crews, the drivers huddled under the overpass with doors half-open, bodies frozen. No one spoke. No one looked away.

The van yawed sideways, then spun, crossing lanes that no longer meant anything. I couldn't tell if the driver had already gotten out or if someone was still inside, trapped.

I leaned forward, trying to see through the rain and spray. The windows were dark. The van kept spinning, rolling in the current. Then, for just a second, it turned at an angle where I could see into the cab.

Movement.

Someone was in there.

An older man. Still at the wheel. That's all I could make out through the rain and spray—gray or white hair, hunched forward, gripping the steering wheel. The van hit the center barrier just ahead of us with a sickening crunch. He didn't let go. Even as the van twisted and spun in the current, I could see him holding on, like steering still mattered.

It didn't. The van was just debris now, same as everything else in that water.

We watched him go—watched as the water carried the van forward, gathering speed until it slammed into the next barrier with a sound that carried even over the storm. The vehicle lurched, shuddered, and then the current took it. Gone.

My heart was hammering. Adrenaline flooded my system—sharp, electric, immediate. My hands were already moving before my brain caught up. I emptied my pockets onto the dash without thinking. Phone. Wallet. Keys. Everything that would weigh me down or get destroyed.

Jane watched me with wide eyes. She'd already figured it out.

"The plan?" she asked finally, her voice slow and cautious. She already knew. She just didn't want to hear it.

"I'm going after them."

"How?" she asked, though her tone said she'd already guessed the answer.

My mouth was dry. My pulse was in my ears. But my hands were steady. That's what mattered. When your body goes quiet while your mind screams, you know you're operating on something deeper than thought.

I'd felt this before. Not often. But enough times to recognize it. The moment when everything narrows to a single point and hesitation burns away. Car wrecks. Burning buildings. Moments where someone was about to die and you were the only one close enough to do something about it.

Most people freeze. Not because they don't care—because they don't know where to start. The chaos is too big. The risk too obvious. They wait for someone else to move first.

I never could.

I looked at Jane. "I have to try."

She went pale, lips parting as the reality landed. Before she could speak—before I could second-guess—I was already moving.

The door swung open and rain sliced across my face. Cold. Sharp. The wind tried to shove me back, but I leaned into it, feet skidding on slick asphalt as I ran for the center divider. My boots splashed through standing water. The roar of the storm swallowed everything else.

I climbed onto the center concrete divider, boots slipping on wet cement. From that height, the water looked different—faster, thicker, less like a river and more like a moving wall. Debris churned through it. The current had teeth.

The van was still spinning off to my left—still taking hits, still being thrown like it could come apart at any second. It wasn't close. Not close enough to reach on my own.

There was no clean entry. No safe angle. Just cold math: the current was faster than I could swim. I needed it to carry me.

I jumped.

The water hit hard—colder than I expected, dark, heavy, immediate. It swallowed my legs and yanked me sideways before I could fully orient myself. The shock stole my breath. My chest seized. For a second, I couldn't tell which way was up.

Then survival kicked in. I forced my head above the surface, gasping, arms thrashing to keep position. The current pulled at me, dragging me downstream. Debris tore past—twisted metal, broken lumber, pieces of lives ripped loose and flung forward. A branch the size of my arm missed my head by inches.

Any of it could end this before it began.

The cold was immediate and brutal. Not numbing—sharp. It bit into my skin, my muscles, made every movement harder. My clothes were already soaked, heavy, pulling me down. I kicked hard, trying to angle toward the van.

Then I heard the shout.

"We're close!"

It wasn't the wind or the water or the thunder. It was Corey.

I barely turned—just enough to see him beside me, forcing his way through the same brutal current, face set with grim determination. Water streamed off his hair, his shoulders. He didn't ask. He didn't hesitate. He just came.

Relief hit me like a physical thing. I wasn't alone in this.

We swam hard, fighting the current, letting it carry us when we had to, angling toward the van. My arms burned. My lungs screamed for more air than I could pull in. The water kept trying to flip me, drag me under, slam me into something solid.

The van pitched and rolled in the whirlpool ahead, a wreck running out of time. Metal groaned with each impact. The rear window had already blown out. Water poured inside.

We were close now. Close enough to see the damage—the crumpled side panels, the shattered glass, the way the whole vehicle listed to one side like it was taking on water.

I reached out, fingers brushing cold metal, then grabbed the rear bumper.

The bumper was already torn up from slamming into the barriers. Sharp edges cut into my palms immediately. I felt the sting, then warmth as blood started flowing, mixing with the cold water. But I didn't let go. If I did, the current would take the van and we'd lose him.

Corey's hand locked down next to mine. Same grip. Same risk. We didn't say anything. Didn't need to.

We had the van—and that's when the real fight started.

The current slammed us against the back of the van again and again. No footing, no leverage. Just two men clinging to a drifting slab of metal in a river that could crush us without even noticing. The impacts drove the air from my lungs. My ribs ached. My shoulders screamed.

"We need bottom," I gasped, spitting water.

He understood immediately.

The only way to move the van was to drop into the current, groping blindly for the riverbed. Every heartbeat counted—one slip, one missed hold, and the van could be gone.

I drew a deep breath and dropped my legs. The current twisted me violently, slammed me sideways, spun me like a ragdoll. My feet swept through nothing but darkness, debris, and the relentless push of water. Something solid hit my shin—hard enough to make me see stars. I kept searching.

Then, finally, grit and stone pressed against my soles.

There.

The relief was immediate but fleeting. The riverbed was slick, unstable. Rocks shifted under my weight. But it was something. Enough to push against.

Corey dropped beside me. I felt him brace, felt his weight settle. We both knew: if one of us let go, we'd both lose the van.

We dug our feet in, trying to find traction on the slick pavement beneath the water. The current pulled at our legs, tried to knock us off balance. I felt the water rising—up to my knees, then my thighs, then my waist. Cold. Fast. Relentless.

My hands were already numb. Blood from the cuts had turned the water around my wrists pink. I couldn't feel my fingers anymore—just pressure where they gripped the bumper.

"On three," I shouted over the roar. "One. Two. Three—"

We shoved. Hard. Every muscle engaged. Legs burning, back straining, hands screaming from the torn metal cutting deeper. The van didn't budge. Not an inch.

It felt like pushing a building. The water pressure against the side of the van was immense. The current fought us with every ounce of force it had.

"Again!" I yelled.

We reset. Planted our feet as best we could. Shoved again. This time the van rocked slightly, just enough to feel it shift in the current. A crack in the river's grip.

"It's moving!" Corey shouted.

We pushed again. And again. My hands were slipping—too much blood, too much water. I couldn't tell if I still had a good grip or if I was just holding on through willpower. My arms shook. My legs threatened to give out. My lungs screamed for more air than I could pull in between waves. The current kept hitting us, trying to sweep our feet out from under us.

Each shove sent shockwaves of pain up my arms, through my shoulders, into my spine. My lower back felt like it was tearing. My thighs burned. My calves cramped.

But the van was moving. Slowly. Inch by inch. The tires found something—pavement, concrete, anything solid enough to catch. It scraped forward, grinding against whatever was beneath it. The sound was horrible—metal on stone, high-pitched and grinding.

"Keep going!" Corey's voice was raw, strained. He was hurting too. I could hear it.

We didn't stop. Couldn't stop. Just kept pushing, resetting, pushing again. The river fought us the whole way, throwing more debris, more water, more force against the van. A plastic cooler slammed into my shoulder. A piece of lumber scraped past my head. The water surged higher for a moment, rising to my chest, trying to lift me off my feet.

But we had momentum now. Small. Fragile. But real.

The van crawled toward the outer bank. Not fast. Not smooth. But moving. Every foot felt like a mile. Every second stretched. My vision started to tunnel. Black edges creeping in. I shook my head, trying to clear it, and kept pushing.

One final heave. The van shuddered, groaned, and slid free of the current's strongest pull, coming to rest on the shoulder. A precarious, trembling victory.

We didn't let go. Not until we were certain it would hold. Not until the river had no power over it anymore. My hands stayed locked on the bumper even after the van stopped moving. It took effort to release my grip. My fingers didn't want to straighten.

The roar of wind and rain hadn't vanished—the storm still raged around us—but the immediate danger had passed. The van was out. The man was safe.

And then the sound of human voices rose above it.

Horns. Shouts. Clapping.

First responders spilled from their vehicles under the overpass, hands raised, faces caught between disbelief and relief. People we hadn't even realized were watching. For a moment, the storm seemed to loosen its grip.

I could barely stand. My legs shook. Water streamed off me. I was cold in a way I'd never been cold before—deep, bone-level cold that made my teeth chatter.

The driver's door creaked open. The old man stumbled out, nearly fell, caught himself on the door frame. He was soaked, shaking, face pale. He looked at us—really looked—and his expression crumbled. He buried his face in his hands, shoulders shaking.

"You saved our lives," he whispered.

The words hit me harder than the water had. Made it real in a way the action hadn't.

Without thinking, I stepped forward and hugged him. He embraced me tightly, shuddering, his whole body trembling. He smelled like river water and fear and something else—gratitude, maybe, though I'd never thought gratitude had a smell before. In that instant, the enormity of the moment landed. He knew, fully, that we had saved his life.

In the back, his wife clutched their dog tightly, tears streaming down her face. The dog—a small terrier, soaked and shaking—licked her chin. Her whispered thanks cut through the chaos, soft and fragile.

"Thank you. Thank you. Oh God, thank you."

I couldn't find words. Just nodded.

I glanced at Corey. He looked like I felt—exhausted, soaked, hands torn up, but standing. We locked eyes for a second. No smile. No celebration. Just acknowledgment.

"We're a rescue organization," I said, low and steady. The words came out with certainty I hadn't expected. But they felt right. True in a way nothing else had in months.

"Yes, we are," he replied, that same unwavering certainty in his voice.

It wasn't a beginning. It wasn't an ending. It was just a fact—finally spoken out loud, undeniable, unshakable.

Soon, other first responders reached a point just above the freeway. They began descending the embankment deliberately, carefully, until they reached the couple. The responders surrounded them, guiding them steadily up and away from danger. One of them draped a thermal blanket over the man and woman's shoulders, asking questions we couldn't hear, moving them to safety.

Corey and I didn't wait. We turned, moving in the opposite direction, boots sloshing through standing water, blood still seeping from the cuts on our hands. No words passed between us. No debrief was needed.

We walked back along the shoulder, climbing toward higher ground. Within minutes, as the storm began to ease and the water receded, Jane met us at the top of the bank. She stood outside the SUV, arms crossed, staring at us like we'd just materialized from another dimension. When we got close enough, she shook her head slowly.

"You two are absolutely insane," she said. But she was smiling. "Get in. You're both going to freeze to death."

We climbed into the SUV. The heat was already running. It felt like heaven.

For a long moment, none of us spoke. Just sat there, breathing, listening to the storm now subsiding outside, feeling the warmth slowly return to our bodies.

Then Corey leaned his head back against the seat and let out a long breath.

"Well," he said quietly. "That happened."

I looked down at my hands. The cuts were deeper than I'd thought. Blood still oozed from a few of them. They'd need cleaning. Probably stitches.

But we'd done it. We'd pulled them out.

Jane put the SUV in gear and pulled away slowly, carefully navigating around debris and pockets of standing water. The rain had eased. Behind us, emergency lights still flashed. The first responders were hard at work, helping the couple, doing what they had to do.

Ahead of us, somewhere in the dark and the storm, waited whatever came next. We had accomplished our goal.

8

Building Discipline

THAT FIRST NIGHT BACK, I sat at my desk. The room was quiet. I pulled up a blank document but didn't start typing. Instead, I let my mind run through everything that had happened in Oklahoma. The storm. The people we'd reached. The ones we hadn't. The elderly couple in the van.

One thing settled in hard: I could do this work. I should do this work. But I couldn't just keep stumbling into it unprepared.

What we'd done in Oklahoma—jumping into that flood—had worked. But it could have easily gone the other way. We got lucky. The current could have taken us. The debris could have killed us. We could have made things worse instead of better. That kind of recklessness might feel like heroism in the moment, but it's not sustainable. It's not professional. And it's not fair to the people depending on you.

I'd learned something crucial: instinct gets you through one crisis. Discipline gets you through a hundred.

No more winging it. No more improvising through chaos. If I was going to do this work, I had to do it right.

Most people think humanitarian work is simple. Show up, hand out supplies, leave. Rescue work isn't like that. It's half instinct, half logistics, all chaos. You're stepping into situations that don't care if you're ready.

I wasn't naive enough to think passion could replace preparation. Excitement fades. What lasts is discipline. If HARP was going to be more than just an idea, it needed structure. A foundation that could hold weight.

***

Two people reached out within the first month. They'd heard about what we'd done in Oklahoma through mutual friends trying to help get the organization off the ground.

Both were eager. Both had good resumes. One had military experience but couldn't stop talking about himself. The other had medical training but froze up when things got uncertain.

I met them separately. Kept the conversations casual. Watched how they talked about risk. One dismissed it entirely. The other tried to control everything.

Neither asked what would happen if something went wrong.

That bothered me more than any lack of skills.

Rescue work isn't built on confidence. It's built on judgment. The ability to pause. To listen. To accept limits without getting angry about them. Sitting there with each of them, I realized that competence without humility was just another liability.

I didn't invite either of them back.

No confrontation. No explanation. I told myself I'd revisit the decision later when the structure was stronger. But the truth was simpler: if I couldn't trust someone to handle uncertainty without ego or rigidity, I couldn't trust them when things went sideways.

That night, the apartment felt quieter than usual. Not relief—loss. I was choosing to stay small deliberately. Turning people away.

It was the first time I understood that building HARP would mean disappointing people long before it helped anyone.

***

I opened a new document and typed the least exciting question possible: What does a rescue team actually need to function?

The list grew fast. Gear. Training. Communications. Medical equipment. Logistics. Clear roles. Funding. A reason for anyone to trust us. Qualified volunteers.

It was almost funny how many things had to line up before we could operate with more than two people.

People imagine this work in snapshots. A rescuer carrying someone through rubble. A helicopter overhead. A photo of hope. They don't see the reality: kneeling on a dirt floor, repacking kits for the fiftieth time because one wrong tool or dead battery could cost someone their life.

I didn't want to be the person showing up with good intentions and bad preparation. Disaster zones don't forgive that. Not war zones, not floods, not collapsed buildings.

You usually get one shot. Everything has to work right the first time. The only way to make that happen is training. Drills. Repetition. Doing it over and over until it's baked deep into your muscle memory.

I pulled every pack I owned onto the floor. Gear from old jobs, old missions, pieces of my past I thought I was done with. I laid it all out and questioned every item. Why this knife? Why this radio? Why this tourniquet? What melts in heat? What fails in cold? What breaks under stress?

I wasn't building a brand. I was building a lifeline. And lifelines don't get second chances.

The problem was obvious: disasters are chaos. No plan survives first contact. But chaos doesn't excuse being unprepared. We needed structure that could bend without breaking.

I started mapping out a training plan. Rope systems. Medical protocols. Communications. Vehicle recovery. Navigation under pressure. Extraction techniques. Disaster psychology. Cultural awareness. Team dynamics.

Some of it I knew. Most of it I needed to learn better. Rescue work wasn't just running into danger. It was running into danger with enough skill to avoid making things worse.

Then there was funding.

Most people think starting a nonprofit means writing proposals, sending polished emails, convincing strangers to give you money. I could have done that. Spent weeks crafting pitches, making promises I wasn't ready to keep.

But it felt wrong.

The truth is, rescue work doesn't translate well to spreadsheets. Unlike organizations that hand out supplies you can photograph, most of what we did couldn't be documented.

High-risk situations don't allow time for media teams. One distraction could cost a life. And often, the people we helped didn't want recognition. Their identities needed protection. Their stories stayed private.

Asking for donations on a "trust me" basis is infinitely harder than showing receipts and photos proving your money went somewhere specific.

So I decided to fund it myself first.

Every dollar I could spare went into gear, communications, training. I didn't know exactly how it would all work out, but I believed in the mission enough to risk it. I wanted HARP to have a foundation I could stake my name on. A record of integrity nobody could question.

This wasn't reckless. It was commitment.

Every pack, every radio, every hour of research and testing I funded myself proved I was all in. Not just believing—doing. Not just for me, but for the people I'd eventually bring into HARP. The team that would depend on me as much as I depended on them.

I wanted HARP's first steps to be honest in every choice. We weren't chasing attention or applause. We were building capability. Building trust. And if we could prove it worked first, others might believe enough to join. But not before.

***

It wasn't a sudden decision. It was years of preparation I hadn't recognized as preparation.

I grew up fascinated by chaos. My father was in law enforcement, my mother in banking—structure was their world. Mine was the opposite. I climbed fences, skated through empty malls at midnight, pushed toward extremes not for the thrill but to see what I could survive. Loss found me early—my first love died in a car accident, the second one betrayed me. Life taught me fast that it was random and cruel, and the only response was to live deliberately. Undercover work, journalism, war reporting—all different ways to test myself against chaos. A pattern emerged: I wasn't chasing money. I was chasing meaning.

When I was younger, I wrote a piece of software that calculated my probability of existing. One specific man meeting one specific woman, conceiving at the exact moment, the right atmospheric conditions, evolutionary timelines—everything that had to align perfectly. The result: one in 40 trillion. That's a four followed by thirteen zeros. Most people can't even process odds that extreme. But I sat there staring at it, trying to understand what it meant. One in 40 trillion chances I was here. Breathing. Thinking. Alive. I wasn't going to waste that.

Every choice I'd made pointed the same direction: toward meaning, toward purpose, toward using every second I'd been given. HARP wasn't a departure from that pattern. It was the culmination of it. I didn't need applause. I didn't need approval. I needed integrity, preparation, backbone. Every reckless choice, every hard lesson, every loss, every skill learned—it all led here.

I leaned back in my chair. The excitement was still there, but quieter now. Steadier. It had turned into resolve. I wasn't rushing. I wasn't forcing anything. I was building. Brick by brick. Decision by decision.

Define the mission. Define roles. Define gear. Define training. Define standards. Define boundaries. Define the why.

Purpose gave me the spark. Discipline would build the fire.

9

World Savior

I MET UP WITH a handful of friends and volunteers at a small dive bar down the street. By this point, we'd completed almost half a dozen operations—not many, but enough to recognize patterns, enough to know what to expect. Each mission had sharpened our approach, tested the teams, pushed our limits. A few people had joined because they believed in the work, and enough donors had come together to form a modest base. I used my social media following to pull in support. Most of the volunteers did the same.

The dive bar had become our makeshift war room. An L.A. institution—walls lined with faded photos of celebrities, magicians, forgotten karaoke stars. Decades of cigarette smoke baked into the walls despite the ban. A neon Budweiser sign cast red light across our table. Someone had ordered a round. My bottle was already sweating in my hand, the label peeling under my thumb.

There was no celebration. No clinking glasses. No noise loud enough to drown out what we were about to do.

We sat together, shoulders heavy with what we'd seen—and what we knew we were about to see again. News from Haiti had hit before we even walked in. Another catastrophe. Another place torn apart. Another reminder that we were all one phone call away from the next disaster.

Someone had pulled up footage on their phone. The screen glowed blue in the dim bar. We passed it around the table in silence. Flattened buildings. Flooded streets. People wading through chest-deep water carrying whatever they could save. My jaw tightened watching it. Throat went dry. It was 2016, and Haiti had been hit again.

A few years earlier, an earthquake had ripped through the same country, toppling buildings and killing somewhere between 220,000 and 316,000 people, depending on who you asked. A place that broken could never fully rebuild. They never recovered much of what was lost—people, infrastructure, entire neighborhoods.

When they rebuilt, they tried to learn. Metal instead of concrete, hoping the flexibility would absorb tremors instead of collapsing. A rational defense against a world that didn't care about reason.

Then nature came back. A hurricane tore through, and the metal meant to protect became a weapon. Sheets ripped from rooftops, twisted into blades that cut through the air and through anything in their path. The hurricane killed over 500 people on the first day, displaced 150,000, and left more than 1.4 million needing aid. Numbers so large they stop meaning anything, leaving only a kind of burning numbness behind.

I used to blame people for not caring about disasters like this. But by then I'd realized: most people can't handle what we were about to walk into. Not physically. Not mentally. And that was fine. We didn't need most people. We needed the few who could.

Still, finding committed volunteers had become almost impossible. We were living in an age where everyone was told they had problems—even when they didn't. Life coaches, self-help gurus, therapists all selling the idea that nobody was living their "best life," that everyone needed healing, that personal growth meant obsessing over every minor discomfort. Capable people who could have done real work got stuck worrying about issues they never had until someone convinced them those issues existed. It drained the pool of volunteers. Made finding good people harder. And it taught me something important: the ones who did show up—the rare few who ignored all that noise and just acted—those were the only ones who mattered.

Some came wide-eyed, overwhelmed, unsure what they were stepping into, but determined to help. Others jumped in believing that saving people would somehow save themselves—a dangerous equation, and one that chaos exposes fast. The river, the rubble, the fire—none of it cares about your intentions. It doesn't make allowances for ego or hope. It strips you bare.

But the ones who approached carefully, who watched and listened, who asked the right questions and accepted their limits—they eventually found the rhythm. The work taught them to measure fear against skill, to turn hesitation into observation, to translate uncertainty into action.

There's a phenomenon in this work, often called the "Savior complex." It happens to some people who step into rescue or humanitarian work and, after saving others—or even just helping—start seeing themselves as saviors. It's not just pride or ego. It's a psychological shift where helping becomes the measure of self-worth, and the person you were before gets overshadowed by the person your ego demands you become.

It's almost like a mental break. Suddenly, every decision, every action, every risk gets filtered through feeding that self-image. The danger is it erodes focus, clarity, judgment—the very things that make someone effective in high-stakes situations. People caught in it start prioritizing the appearance of heroism over the actual mission. They take risks not because they're necessary, but because the narrative in their head demands a performance.

One ego-driven decision can cost lives.

The most experienced rescuers I've met recognize it immediately. It's a quiet but dangerous shift, a temptation to measure your value by the number of people you "save" instead of the discipline, planning, and skill it actually takes to do the work safely and effectively.

I'd witnessed this firsthand a few months earlier during an operation. We were assessing a site from a safe distance, noting debris, water flow, weak points in the soil, when a small team from another humanitarian organization arrived ahead of us. They were there to distribute supplies—food, water, blankets. At first, they moved carefully, picking their steps along unstable ground.

One of their volunteers—young, eager, completely untrained for this terrain—spotted a woman trapped in a car just off the edge of the slide. Without thinking, he ran forward.

His boots hit loose soil and slipped immediately. Dirt cascaded down the slope. He grabbed at branches, at debris, anything to keep moving. Shouting her name. The urgency was magnetic but reckless.

My chest tightened. I could feel it—the wrongness of his movement, the ground shifting under his weight. Every step sent small rocks tumbling. Dust rose in clouds. The car groaned, metal settling deeper into the unstable earth.

He reached her and started lifting debris, shouting instructions, completely ignoring the ground beneath him. His movements were fast, decisive, but unmeasured. He wasn't thinking about safety. He wasn't calculating risk. He was performing, driven by the moment and the idea of being the hero.

I watched—and so did everyone with me—our stomachs tight, hands clenched. The smell of disturbed earth and gasoline from the car's ruptured tank in the air. The woman inside wasn't screaming anymore. Just staring at him, wide-eyed.

Every piece of debris he moved risked collapse. One misstep and both he and the woman could have been swept away.

I called out, warning him, but he didn't hear. Ego had taken over, pushing him forward faster than the situation could handle. It was the savior complex in full effect—pride disguised as courage, consuming judgment and reason.

He got her out. Pulled her through the passenger window just as the ground beneath the car's rear tires gave way. The vehicle slid six feet down the slope and stopped, wedged against a boulder. If she'd still been inside, she'd be dead.

By the time the woman was safe, he was still grinning, chest heaving, convinced he'd made the difference. I let him have that moment. But I knew what we'd witnessed: unchecked ego is as dangerous as any physical hazard. Moments like that stick with you. Warnings written in real time.

My heart was still hammering when we walked away.

Back in the bar, we sat quietly, piecing together a plan from scraps of information. Hours had passed. Empty bottles accumulated on the table between us. My back ached from the wooden chair. The neon sign buzzed overhead.

It was a reminder that no matter how much you prepare, no matter how hard you fight to rebuild, control is mostly an illusion. Sometimes you search for meaning in the rubble and find nothing. You can rebuild. Try to build better. But nature doesn't care. The world moves on with or without you.

After more discussion and mapping possibilities, we agreed we'd leave the following day for Haiti. The decision felt inevitable, a necessary step forward into uncertainty, guided only by experience, instinct, and the knowledge that action—how-ever imperfect—was the only option.

I pushed back from the table and stood. My legs were stiff. Outside, the L.A. night air hit cool against my skin. I checked my phone—11:47 PM. In less than twelve hours, we'd be packing. Then we'd be gone.

I walked to my car, hands in my pockets, mind already shift-ing to the operation.

10

The Fixer

WE HAD PLANE TICKETS by morning. Becca worked her usual magic. Our small team—five people—was heading to Haiti. We didn't know where we'd fit into the mess, but we trusted we'd figure it out on the ground. By then, we had no illusions about heroism.

The flight blurred by. Turbulence hit like clockwork—as if the sky had it out for us. You'd think I'd be used to it by then, but I wasn't.

We landed in Port-au-Prince. The airport was chaos disguised as importance. Lines stretched forever—people without visas, people trying to get visas, people arguing, pleading, waiting. Becca had anticipated this and submitted our paperwork in advance. We cut through, cleared customs, and stepped into the humid crush of the city.

We were among the first organizations to arrive, though that didn't make me feel better. We grabbed our bags and stepped into the streets—horns blaring, vendors shouting, the city vibrating under its own pulse of urgency.

That's when we met him—a young man in his early-thirties, standing apart from the crowd. He scanned faces, searching.

"Sir... can I help? First time here?" His English was nearly perfect. "I know this land. I know the people. Do you need a fixer?"

A fixer is more than a guide. A fixer is the difference between getting lost and getting home alive. They know the terrain, the unspoken rules, the lines you don't cross. Mercius had that presence. He wasn't loud, but he commanded space. Alert, precise, measured—someone who had survived more than most ever would.

"We're a nonprofit," I said. "Rescue work. I'm sorry, we can't pay."

A slow smile spread across his face. "It's ok. I'll still help. These are my people. Do you need vehicles? Lodging? I know how to get it."

I studied him for a second. There was something solid about him. Not just confidence—competence. The kind of person who knew how things worked here, who could navigate systems I'd never understand. And more importantly, he wanted to help his own people. That mattered.

I extended my hand. "Welcome to the team, Mercius."

He shook it, eyes sharp—not suspicious, just aware. Within minutes, he was on the phone, coordinating. By the time he hung up, two Toyota Hiluxes were on the way and lodging had been arranged.

"There's a lot of work here." He shifted his weight.

I nodded.

The trucks arrived on time, engines rumbling low and steady. We loaded our gear. That's when I noticed them—a man and a woman standing near an exit, five green military duffels at their feet. They looked out of place, scanning the scene like they were waiting for someone to tell them what to do. The bags pinned them there. They couldn't move around easily, couldn't search for help. They were stuck, hoping someone would notice them.

The woman caught me looking. In a place like this, you notice your own kind—people who are new, uncertain, searching.

She murmured to her husband; he nodded, and she approached carefully. Her smile wasn't joy—it was relief. A signal that she was here, willing, even if she didn't yet understand the terrain.

"Hello... American?"

"Yeah," she nodded. "We're from Texas."

"What brings you here?"

"We... just showed up," gesturing to a few of the duffels. "Supplies—school kits, medical, water filters, clothing. We came to help, somehow."

"Where are you headed?"

She hesitated. "That's the problem. We don't know. We were hoping someone could point us in the right direction. Are you with an organization?"

"HARP. Nonprofit. Rescue work."

Her eyes lit up, relief cutting through the tension. "Can we... join you?"

I studied them. They looked nervous but determined. Not the kind of people who'd fold at the first sign of trouble.

"What kind of experience do you have?" I asked.

"My husband's a firefighter. Twenty years. I'm an EMT."

That changed things. Not volunteers playing hero—actual trained professionals.

"Ever worked in conditions like this?"

"No," she admitted. "But we know how to follow protocol. We know when to listen. And we know when we're in over our heads."

That was the answer I needed. Not ego. Not overconfidence. Just honesty and skill.

I looked at the other duffles. "What's in those?"

Medical supplies mostly," she said. "Bandages, antibiotics, water purification, basics. We brought what we could carry. Actually, more than we can carry.

I nodded. They had training we could use. Supplies we needed. And—most importantly—they understood their limits. That humility mattered more than experience.

"All right," I said. "Welcome aboard."

She went back to get her husband, and together they hauled their gear to the trucks.

On the road, Mercius told us where we'd be staying: a well-known hotel at the center of Port-au-Prince, where most humanitarian workers gathered. Twenty minutes later, we rolled through its gates. Bags came off fast. I'd been texting Becca, and by the time we reached the front doors, she'd already booked rooms for all of us—including the new arrivals.

Inside, the hotel felt different than I expected. Aid workers, journalists, and a few early diplomats were already staking their ground. Even with just a handful of people, you could feel it—the calculations behind polished smiles, the measured handshakes, the careful nods.

Within days, this place would be packed. Right now, it was just the early wave—the ones who got here fast, who had connections, who knew how to move. And already, the games had started.

Someone was always watching. Not because you were a threat, but because you might have something they needed: contacts, resources, information. Nonprofits live or die by the donation dollar, and donations are brutal business. A headline, a viral image, a compelling clip—these could mean the difference between securing a grant, landing a whale donor, or shutting down.

Sabotage wasn't rare. It was routine. Competing nonprofits—supposed allies—undercutting each other for visibility, credit, recognition. I'd seen organizations approach after the fact, asking to buy footage, wanting to claim credit for work they hadn't done.

This hotel wasn't a place to rest. It was a marketplace—alliances traded, information hoarded, motives disguised.

It's a strange feeling, being surrounded by people who all have reasons for being here—and knowing not all those reasons are about helping. The reporters need footage. The NGO workers need metrics for their donors. Everyone's building something: a career, a reputation, a grant proposal. Even the ones doing good work have to play the game—sell the suffering, package the tragedy, make it compelling enough that someone back home opens their wallet.

I'm not saying it's all cynical. Some of it's necessary. But standing there, watching people angle for the best shot of devastation, it's hard not to feel like disaster has become a business. And the people suffering? They're the product.

***

That night, we gathered outside around a small fire at the back hotel patio. We laid out all the gear—ropes, medical kits, radios, protective equipment—and went through it piece by piece.

Everyone checked their own supplies while we walked them through equipment they might not have used before. Knots tied, radios tested, medical kits inspected. We corrected small errors, demonstrated techniques, answered questions. No lectures, no judgment—just clear, careful instruction.

By the time the fire had burned down to embers, everyone knew their gear, knew what was expected, knew how to use what they had.

We didn't linger. The night was long. We turned in as the fire died behind us.

***

The next morning, we got up early and headed downstairs for breakfast.

The place had filled overnight. Somewhere between midnight and dawn, the hotel had swollen with bodies—journalists, reporters, volunteers, the newly arrived and the freshly shaken. All funneled into the same buffet line that now stretched nearly out the door.

We joined it.

The breakfast buffet was chaos—a low-grade riot disguised as hospitality. Plates clattered, silverware scraped, people bumped into each other without apology. Tension filled the air.

Everyone looked exhausted. Brittle. Volunteers, aid workers, journalists—they all had the same stare. Half seemed intent on saving the world. The other half, on saving themselves.

We were almost done eating when Mercius appeared in the front doorway.

There was something in his eyes—sharp, quick, like someone who'd slept with one ear open his entire life. He scanned the room with hardened instinct, the kind you develop by surviving.

His smile wasn't arrogance, and it wasn't friendly. It was armor. Here, you keep moving, keep talking, keep smiling—or the city swallows you whole.

"The trucks are staged outside," he said, English laced with French and Creole.

His eyes surveyed the room, calculating. Not suspicious—strategic. He was mapping us, deciding where we fit, what use we might be, what trouble we might bring. This wasn't his first time. He knew the game. He knew most couldn't be trusted, and those who could had to be weeded out slowly, cautiously. He was looking for authenticity.

"Where do you want to go first?"

I wiped the last bit of eggs from my plate and set my fork down. "Not sure yet. Suggestions? Based on what you know about the damage."

He paused. Stared for a long beat—too long to be casual. Something behind his expression shifted, as if deciding whether to trust me with what he was about to say. His easy smile thinned.

"There's a place across the river. A remote village," he finally said. "No one's attempted it. I was told about it last night."

"Why not?"

"There's no way to get across," he said. "There was a small footbridge—gone. Washed away. That river wasn't even there before the storm. It cut a new path, isolated the village completely."

"How many people?"

"A few hundred, I think." He swallowed, the words dragging something out of him. "Injuries. Homes gone. Some buried. Men, women and children missing."

The mask slipped just enough to reveal the truth: he cared. More than he wanted us to notice.

I sat with it for a moment, weighing the risks, the unknowns. No road. No bridge. No guarantees.

"How deep is the river?"

He hesitated. "I don't know."

I nodded. "All right. Let's go there."

His expression froze briefly—questioning whether I was serious. Once he realized I meant it, his posture shifted slightly. He didn't smile, but something in him accepted what came next.

He knew I wasn't bluffing. And he knew we were going.

11

Hells Kitchen

ONCE WE CLEARED THE city and cut through the back roads, Mercius glanced over as we approached a roadblock—or what passed for one. Smoldering tires, twisted metal, debris dragged across the pavement. A jumble that could shred tires or flip a truck if we weren't careful. The air was thick with smoke, stinging my eyes and throat, carrying the faint smell of something burned beyond recognition.

In Haiti, these blockades meant something. Sometimes they were protests—locals slowing traffic, making a point. Other times, they were traps. Set to stop a vehicle long enough for a gang to swarm it, armed and ready, stripping everything: cargo, equipment, people.

We parked a fair distance back watching the smoke rise. I wasn't about to gamble on which version this was. This wasn't "maybe a problem." This was immediate. Real. I turned to Mercius.

"Another route."

He watched the flames for a moment. "There is only one other option. We cut through a place called Hell's Kitchen."

I let the name settle.

He didn't look at me when he continued. "If we go that way, the trucks keep moving. No stops. The women stay low in their seats, heads down, out of sight. If we look like we know where we're going, we should be fine."

"But this," he nodded toward the smoke, "this is different. Here, they want you to stop. Once you stop, you belong to whoever's waiting."

Hell's Kitchen—inside La Saline, a neighborhood in Port-au-Prince—wasn't so much a neighborhood as a living thing. Unpredictable. Moving to a rhythm you had to respect or pay for ignoring. Streets shifted by the hour. Rules were invisible. Anything could be bought if you knew the right people—or if you were willing to accept the consequences.

Crowds pressed in from all sides. The air smelled like rot, sweat, and diesel, mixed with something older—something that clung to your clothes long after you drove away. The danger wasn't the noise or the number of people. It was what people did to survive here. They turned scarcity into opportunity. Hustlers worked the streets with smiles that looked friendly until you realized they weren't. Traders sold anything—water, food, information—at prices that shifted depending on how desperate you looked. And some people didn't bother hiding what they did. Their work was brutal, and they made no apologies for it.

A bag of food could be leverage. A jug of water could have strings attached. In a place like that, the line between a deal and a disaster could collapse in seconds.

I tapped my fingers on the steering wheel, thinking.

"Any other way in besides Hell's Kitchen?"

"No." Not a hint of doubt.

Something in his voice—a hesitation, maybe. An acknowledgment that he was asking us to walk into a place built to consume anyone unprepared. He wasn't offering options. He was giving us the courtesy of choosing something already decided.

We were going through Hell's Kitchen. No way around it.

Mercius didn't want to be there any more than I did. We'd settled on a plan during the drive, but plans didn't mean much once you crossed into a place like this. Safety wasn't on the table. What mattered was how we looked moving through it.

The women stayed low in the trucks, tucked behind bags and gear, outlines hidden in shadow. The men stayed upright, faces blank, eyes on the road ahead. Whatever rose on either side, we wouldn't acknowledge it.

Eyes forward.

Hell's Kitchen announced itself before we saw it. The trucks shuddered over broken pavement. Buildings leaned into the roadway, walls carrying years of grime and survival. Pavement cracked in long seams, patched and re-patched until the repairs became part of the street itself.

The sound never stopped. Engines strained. Vendors shouted over each other. Distant arguments threaded through the noise. Metal scraped metal. People moved with quick, precise steps—consequences already memorized. Vendors pushed carts stacked with fruit or salvaged goods. Children weaved through them, silent, alert. Survival wasn't a strategy here. It was reflex.

The unsettling part wasn't the shouts or the number of bodies. It was the eyes. They tracked us from doorways, carts, alleys narrow enough to miss if you weren't looking. The looks weren't curious. They measured. Took inventory.

We stuck to the plan. Trucks kept a steady pace, tires grinding over last night's trash fires. Heat rose off the piles and drifted across the road in thin, wavering sheets. People gathered around mounds of discarded objects—electronics stripped to metal skeletons, broken tools, fabric worn to threads. Anything with a trace of use had been pulled apart and bartered before we arrived. What remained was the residue of a life built entirely on making do.

We eased through, careful with each turn, trucks rocking over uneven ground. Behind the wheel, tension pressed in—the quiet calculation behind every stare, the sense that this place didn't need to swallow you whole to make you disappear. It could erase you one moment at a time.

Still, we kept moving. Eyes forward. No pauses. No second looks.

The streets began to thin. Buildings fell away behind us, the crush of bodies easing with each block. The noise faded—first the shouts, then the metal scraping, then the engines straining over trash. Within minutes, Hell's Kitchen was in the rearview mirror, and the road opened ahead of us.

Finally, space. Real space. The road hugged the coastline, a ribbon of asphalt between fractured hills and turquoise water. The sea was impossibly clear, but its beauty couldn't erase the hurricane's damage: overturned boats, roofs torn from moorings, trees uprooted, debris scattered across sand. Paradise and devastation side by side.

Mercius sat next to me, eyes on the road while keeping watch on the second vehicle. Corey drove that truck, hands tight on the wheel, eyes shifting between potholes and coastline.

The streets were barely recognizable—jagged gaps, scattered debris, collapsed sections. He maneuvered each obstacle carefully, aware that every misstep could be costly. Even with all that focus, I saw him stealing glances at the water, letting the color and curve of sand pull at him for just a second.

The women in my truck sat upright, heads turning toward the water. Each seemed to sense the balance—awe mixed with the reminder that beauty here was paid for in loss. White sand, turquoise waves, tattered palms. All of it carried something no photograph could capture.

Haiti has always been a land of contradictions. Its history bleeds into everything, from coral cliffs to cities on steep hills. The first Black republic, forged in rebellion, still carrying debt imposed by France, decades of political chaos, foreign interventions leaving deep scars. Every village, every shattered roof, carried echoes of that struggle. Reminders of people who survived centuries of upheaval yet remain vulnerable to nature and circumstance.

The road curved along the coastline, hurricane damage visible in every fractured wall and twisted beam. Yet even here, pockets of resilience appeared. Some homes had been rebuilt with salvaged materials. Tin roofs patched. Walls leaning but standing. Palm fronds shimmered green and gold despite being shredded. Small groups moved deliberately through sand and streets—children barefoot, women carrying water, men salvaging from wreckage. Life persisted. Fragile but defiant.

I kept an eye on Corey's truck. His careful weaving, steady hands, reminded me that convoy safety depended on both trucks moving as one. One misstep could send us into the ruins. Both he and I kept the rhythm.

Even with this fragile peace, tension lingered. Every ruined home, every palm twisted by wind and water told a story of what could vanish in an instant. Yet for this stretch of road, the moment held. The convoy moved forward. Engines humming.

Hours passed in silence. Some passengers slept, heads tilted. Others stayed awake, stuck in their own thoughts, watching the coastline blur past broken roads.

I sank into my own mind. Thought about childhood. Life taken for granted—the warmth of home, certainty of food, safety so constant it became invisible until it was gone. Luxuries that shaped the person I'd become.

I wondered: if any of those pieces had been missing—uncertainty instead of stability, fear instead of freedom, hunger instead of plenty—would I even be here now? Would I have the patience, the resilience, the ability to step into places like this and make a difference? Or would I be consumed by the same struggle surrounding everyone here?

There's a strange guilt that comes with privilege. People see stability and assume softness. They see comfort and assume ignorance. They see someone who grew up safe and fed and think: *What do you know about suffering? What gives you the right to be here?*

But here's the truth they miss: those things—the full belly, the safe home, the freedom to ask questions without punishment—those aren't weaknesses. They're the foundation that lets you stand steady when everything around you is collapsing. You can't pour from an empty cup. You can't lift someone else when you're still drowning.

The security I grew up with didn't make me soft. It made me capable. It gave me the space to develop judgment, patience, the ability to think clearly under pressure. It taught me I didn't have to fight for every scrap, so I could focus on something bigger than survival.

People resent that. They think because you didn't suffer, you don't deserve to help. That your compassion is somehow lesser because it came from abundance rather than deprivation. As if pain is the only teacher that matters.

But in these places, watching people who'd been dealt impossible hands, I understood: my privilege wasn't something to apologize for. It was something to use. The stability that shaped me was exactly what allowed me to step into instability and not crumble. The comfort I'd known gave me the strength to sit with discomfort without flinching.

The people we were helping now were mirrors of what we might have been under different circumstances. But they were also the reason our hands were steady enough to reach out in the first place.

I glanced at the men and women around me. Each of us was here because life had made us who we were. Each carried privilege—not always wealth or comfort, but opportunity, experience, perspective. And each had a choice: let it fade into comfort, or turn it into action.

Privilege, stability, opportunity—they're raw materials. Some people squander them. Others use them to sustain, protect, restore. We're shaped by what we're given. The real test is what we do with it.

The sun slid lower over the water, casting a thin golden light across the coastline. For a moment, the trucks seemed suspended in time, moving through a world both beautiful and broken.

The thought settled quietly: maybe being alive isn't just about surviving. Maybe it's about carrying forward what you've been given to lift someone else, somewhere else, out of the wreckage.

12

Sixty Children

Hours had passed. A 190-mile drive that should have taken three hours had stretched to nearly eight. The roads were shattered and relentless, but so far we'd been lucky—no blown tires, no mechanical failures, nothing that could strand a truck.

For most of the drive, we'd barely spoken. Just the hum of the engine, the crunch of gravel, the occasional radio check with Corey. The sun had been high when we left the coast. Now it hung low, casting gold-and-rose light over the hills, glinting off every jagged rock and rain-slicked puddle. Dust rose with each bump, coating the windshield in a thin film I had to keep wiping away.

***

Mercius had been scanning the road for the last hour, leaning forward occasionally, then settling back. Finally, he spoke.

"We're close. There will be a road on the right soon—a cutoff. That'll get us to the village."

He straightened in his seat, eyes on the horizon. Most of the others were asleep, lulled by the fragile calm after hours of tension. Behind us, the second truck held formation. Corey's focus was sharp—hands steady on the wheel, eyes shifting between potholes and the coastline, stealing glimpses of the last light on turquoise water.

A few minutes later, Mercius spoke again. "Here."

A narrow dirt track appeared, more riverbed than road. I slowed. Sharp stones jutted from the earth. Each bump was a warning: a misstep could puncture a tire or throw a truck off balance. Dust thickened the air.

The passengers stirred, rubbing eyes, bracing against the walls. I keyed the radio. "Corey, you read?"

A crackle. "Go for Corey."

"This track will get us to—or as close as possible to—the village."

I glanced at Mercius. "How far?"

He paused. "Usually fifteen minutes to the footbridge. But this road isn't normal. Maybe thirty."

"About thirty minutes."

"Copy. Thirty minutes."

The river appeared, running alongside the road. Water churned over stones, carrying debris—splintered wood, twisted metal, pieces of homes and lives torn apart by the storm. We drove slowly, keeping pace with the current, the trucks grinding forward while the river rushed past.

This river had been born from the hurricane, rushing down from the hills with enough force to reshape the landscape. The last light of the day caught the surface in brief flashes, reflecting into the truck interior, lighting up faces for just a second—everyone quiet, understanding what we were driving toward.

We pressed on. Mercius sat higher in his seat, scanning ahead. The footbridge had crossed a small creek before the hurricane—barely a trickle during dry season, something you could step over. But the storm had turned that creek into a river, swelling it with runoff from the hills, transforming what had been a gentle crossing into a raging torrent. The bridge had been built for a stream. Now it faced a completely different force.

Then he saw it. "The bridge!"

Headlights cut through the dusk. The bridge—fractured, leaning, jagged—was more a memory than a structure. Built for a creek, it had never stood a chance against what the hurricane created.

Corey pulled up alongside. I stepped out, boots crunching on stones, spray hitting my face. The air smelled like mud, rot, and iron from uprooted earth.

"I can see why no one's been able to get to this place," Corey said.

"Yeah," I said, studying the broken concrete. "But we'll find a way."

We waded into the river, testing depth and current. The riverbed dropped unpredictably. Debris floated past—enough to knock a truck off its wheels if we weren't careful.

I stepped back out of the water, boots heavy with mud. Corey did the same. I looked at him, then at Mercius.

"We need to head upriver," I said. "Find a spot where it widens out, where the current's not as strong and the bottom's more stable. This section's too deep and too fast."

Mercius nodded, studying the churning water. "Yes. Further up, the river spreads. It may be shallower there, easier to cross."

"Worth a shot," Corey said.

I climbed into my truck, Corey into his. Mercius settled back into the passenger seat, already scanning upriver through the windshield. Engines rumbled. Dust and gravel lifted as both trucks eased back onto the track. Upriver we went, looking for a crossing that might only exist in the narrow space between hope and disaster.

We continued alongside the river for several minutes, the trucks crunching over uneven stones, dust and mud spraying in our wake. Then the river began to widen. The current spread out, losing some of its violent focus. The roar softened slightly as the water fanned across a broader bed.

I slowed, letting the headlights sweep across the surface, assessing width, depth, flow. Corey pulled up beside me, doing the same. We were both looking for the same thing—a section stable enough to risk.

That's when I heard it. Voices—faint but real, carrying over the water.

"There."

Movement on the far bank caught my eye again. I swept my flashlight across the slope, and more figures appeared—people, standing, waiting, alert but not panicked.

I called for Mercius. He jumped out and walked to my side.

"There are people over there."

I shone the light so he could see. He spoke rapidly in French. A conversation followed, voices rising and falling over the water. When it paused, he turned back to me.

"They're from the village next to the one we're trying to reach. They've put people here to flag anyone who can help. No food, no medical supplies, no clean water. They've been waiting."

I swept the beam across the bank again. Even if we could reach it, the incline was steep—nearly vertical. Getting the trucks up would be impossible. Corey stepped closer, silent, studying the slope.

I turned to Mercius. "We can't get up that bank. Ask if they know of another point where vehicles could climb—somewhere with conditions like this, but with a manageable slope."

Mercius spoke again, faster this time, then turned back to me with something like wonder in his eyes.

"They will dig the bank down."

I blinked. "Dig the bank down... themselves?"

"Yes. So vehicles can get up."

I stared at him for a second, trying to process what he'd just said. In my world, you'd need heavy equipment for this. Excavators. Hours of work. A crew. Here, they were going to do it with shovels and their bare hands. And from the way they talked, they'd already started.

I looked at Corey. He met my gaze, silent, stunned, but steady.

"All right. Let's make it happen."

I turned back to Mercius and nodded.

The river kept roaring. It didn't care what we were trying to do. But for the first time in hours, I thought we might actually pull this off.

I called back to Mercius, who relayed instructions. The people on the opposite bank scattered, moving with purpose. Some disappeared into the darkness, returning moments later with shovels, picks, anything that could move earth. Others started immediately, attacking the slope with their hands.

We had work to do on our side too. As they dug, we repacked the trucks, shifting weight toward the rear to give the tires better traction. The crossing was a long shot, but it was the only option we had. Rain began to fall—fat drops pattering across the cab and river, a reminder that the window of calm could close at any moment.

The work took time. We moved gear, adjusted loads, tested radio communications. The rain kept falling, light but steady. After we'd done everything we could with the trucks, people stepped away to stretch, shake out sore muscles, process what was about to happen.

One woman pulled out a satellite phone, speaking briefly to family before passing it along. Mercius sat on a rock nearby, typing on his own device. I walked over.

"Girlfriend?"

He looked up. "Wife and daughter."

The words caught me off guard. I'd wondered why he was here—why this man, with a family of his own, had chosen to be in this place, risking everything. He read the question on my face.

"You're wondering why I am not with them, especially when no money is involved."

I nodded slowly.

"Because I love my people, my culture. I love my wife and daughter more than I can say. But what kind of man would I be if I stayed home while things broke around me? I am here for them too, in my way. I make this place better for them, even a little. This work—this risk—it's for all of them. For their future."

His words settled into me heavy and real. I thought of my own country, once filled with men who left families to fight, to risk everything for something larger than themselves. Their sacrifices shaped lives, communities, nations. Now, it seemed, the choice was different. Men stayed. They anchored themselves to family, giving everything they could there—but the larger fights, the battles that could change the world outside their doors, those didn't happen anymore.

Here, in this small corner of the world, I saw it in its starkest form: the same desire to protect, to love, to give, but directed inward instead of outward. Mercius had chosen outward anyway. He'd taken the risk most would never consider, carrying not just his own future, but the burden of those who couldn't act for themselves. And in that, there was something both humbling and stirring—a quiet proof that the old ways, the ways that demanded sacrifice for more than immediate comfort, still existed, if only in the few willing to pay the price.

I stepped back, feeling the rain on my face, listening to the muted rush of the river, the faint scraping of tools on earth. This was the work of men who refused to stand idle, who understood that protecting family sometimes meant leaving them, if only for a while, to shape the world around them into something worth returning to.

An hour had passed. The people on the far bank called out, their voices carrying across the water. Mercius answered quickly, his words sharp and deliberate. We trained the flashlight across the river—and froze.

What had been a sheer cliff, impossible for vehicles to climb, had been reshaped. The slope was no longer vertical. It had been turned into a climbable hill, the earth packed and shaped by hands and determination, not machines.

I stood at the water's edge, letting the light sweep over the work. The effort was visible in every contour, every edge smoothed and reinforced. The river still roared, still threatened, but the passage now existed. The impossible had been made possible.

I turned to Corey, who'd been watching in quiet disbelief, the glow of the headlights reflected in his eyes. He shook his head, almost smiling.

"It's done."

"Yes. It's time."

The river waited, indifferent. But for the first time, so did we.

13

Controlled Risk

I TOOK MY TRUCK first. Every ounce of gear had been shifted to the rear, every line of drift calculated. The narrow cut in the far bank was a one-shot target—miss it and the river would pull us downstream into the debris. There was no second chance.

I eased the nose into the current. At first it was a firm push against the bumper, then a steady pull, the river testing the tires, the chassis, the momentum I'd built. The hood stayed above the water. If it dipped under, the engine would flood and die. Water ran along the fenders and up the windshield, blurring the headlights but not killing them.

The current grabbed the truck harder. Water forced its way through the doors, pouring into the cab, seeping through every gap. The floor sloshed beneath my boots, mud and river grit swirling. I gripped the wheel. Mercius braced against the dash, eyes moving between the river outside and my hands on the wheel. Behind us, the bed groaned as gear shifted with every lurch.

The truck rode that fragile line—tires fighting for grip, engine screaming, the current pulling at every part of us. I kept the revs high. The water tried to lift us, shove us sideways. In those seconds, the world was nothing but a fight against the river.

Then the ground changed. The front tires found the center rise—the small patch of high ground that could save us. The truck lurched as momentum met traction. I gave it more throttle. The rear slipped, spraying water high along the cab, then caught again. The truck pitched forward, tires clawing. Water screamed along the sides, trying to tear us loose, but the slope took us—slow at first, then with the force of physics finally working in our favor. Mud and gravel tore at the tires. The engine barked, then steadied. Water poured out from under the chassis, but the truck climbed.

Finally, the slope gave way to solid earth. Tires gripped the bank. The engine dropped to a lower note, steadying. The cab was half-full of river water, but we were across.

We'd made it.

I jumped out, boots squishing in the water draining from the cab. But we weren't done yet. I looked up at the bank the villagers had cut down—the slope they'd dug by hand in the dark. From the water, it had looked manageable. Up close, standing at the base, it looked steep. Rough. Uncertain.

I walked to the front of the truck, studying the angle. Mud and loose earth. No way to know if it would hold under the truck's weight or if the tires would just churn and slip, digging us into a hole we couldn't escape.

Mercius stepped out, following my gaze up the slope. He didn't say anything. Neither did I. We both knew what we were looking at.

I climbed back into the cab. Shifted into low gear. Took a breath.

"Here we go."

I gave it throttle. The truck lurched forward. Tires bit into the loose soil, throwing mud and rocks behind us. The engine roared. For a second, the rear tires spun—sliding, searching for grip. My hands tightened on the wheel.

Then they caught.

The truck surged upward, clawing its way up the grade the villagers had cut. Mud sprayed. The engine screamed. But the slope held. Inch by inch, the truck climbed. The front tires crested the top first, then the rear, and suddenly we were on solid ground.

I killed the engine and sat there for a second, letting it settle. We'd made it.

I jumped out again, raised the flashlight, and swept the beam across the river, yelling over the current.

"We made it! Your turn!"

Corey took a breath I could almost hear from where I stood. His truck nosed into the water, following the same line. The river took hold immediately. Water sheeted over the bumper, climbed the doors, rushed into the cab. The engine cried out, then shifted down. I watched every foot of his fight—the cab shuddering, the tires spinning, the current pulling.

He hit the rise in the center. For a moment, it looked like the river would win. Then, slow and stubborn, the rear caught. His truck inched forward, grinding against the slope, water spilling over the doors, engine whining as he forced it up the bank.

A final push. Tires bit into the earth. The truck pitched forward, climbing, climbing, until it finally rolled up beside us. Steam rose from the hood. Water poured from the doors. And for the first time in hours, we exhaled.

People came from everywhere. Some jumped, shouted, fists raised. Others were quiet, and steady. Mercius spoke quickly to a few men, French flying fast. They nodded, pointed north.

"The village we need is three miles up the road."

I looked around at the crowd gathering—exhausted, wet, carrying what little they'd managed to save. "What about them? Their village?"

"They've moved everyone out. Many are hurt. Many need help. And many..." Mercius let the words hang for a moment. "Many have already died."

I looked at the faces around us again. People who'd just lost everything—homes, loved ones, their entire world reshaped in a single night. And here we were, about to drive past them to reach another village three miles away.

"We'll come back," I said to Mercius. "Once we've done what we can up the road, we come back here. Make sure they know that."

He nodded and spoke quickly to the group in French. A few faces lifted slightly. Not relief—they'd heard promises before. But acknowledgment.

We thanked the helpers, climbed back into the trucks, and pressed forward. I felt the guilt of leaving them behind, but we couldn't help everyone at once. We had to start somewhere.

***

The trucks rumbled back onto what was left of the road. The village was only three miles away, but at this pace—navigating around fallen trees, collapsed walls, sections of road that had simply washed away—it would take time.

Our headlights cut narrow paths through the darkness, showing the damage in brief, brutal flashes. Trees snapped, stripped of leaves, limbs bent at impossible angles. Houses peeled open, roofs torn away, walls reduced to skeletons of wood and concrete. Tin sheeting clung to branches, sharp and flapping in the wind.

People moved through the wreckage, careful, deliberate. Some carried what little they could salvage. Some sat staring at the remains of their lives, mouths slightly open, eyes empty. I saw a woman holding the body of a child, its small form limp in her arms as she rocked back and forth, whispering words I couldn't hear. A man clutched a broken door frame against his chest, as if holding it tight enough could turn it back into a home.

Every foot forward made my chest tighter. I wondered how someone could see this level of destruction over and over. Could the mind truly shield itself? Would the heart harden, or would every loss dig deeper into memory, making even the smallest comforts at home feel temporary, impossible? I felt the pressure of every life in the rubble.

I glanced at the others in the truck. Most had their heads down, staring at their laps, hands curled into fists or drumming on knees. Mercius alone looked out, eyes steady, taking it in with the kind of quiet focus that absorbed everything without breaking.

We kept weaving through debris. Corey's truck stayed tight behind us. I thought about the people with him, what they were seeing. A few were new to this kind of work. Most had never seen devastation like this, where the chaos was raw and unavoidable. In the United States, destruction is often cleaned up fast, covered, contained. Here, it screamed in every direction—demanding you see it, acknowledge it.

Then a flash of movement. A small girl, maybe eight, darted into the road. Joy radiated from her, pure and unrestrained, a sharp contrast to the despair surrounding us. She waved hard, her energy impossible to ignore. For a moment, everything else—the broken homes, the chaos, the loss—fell away.

She reached the side of the truck just as I rolled down the window. Mercius leaned over to speak, but she held up a hand.

"I need no French. These are Americans. I will speak my best English."

Mercius chuckled, shrugging at me.

The girl looked at me, her grin wide, fearless, unbroken. "Follow me to the house. Ok?"

I smiled back. "Ok, I will follow you to the house."

Her eyes lit up. Her grin got even bigger. She turned and skipped ahead, waving for us to follow, weaving through the wreckage like she'd memorized every broken piece.

I followed her. Watching this small girl move through the destruction with that much energy, that much trust in strangers—it cut through everything else. The mud, the splintered wood, the loss all around us. She didn't care. She was just happy we were here.

She led us down what used to be the main road, now barely recognizable under debris and mud. The trucks crawled behind her, engines rumbling low. She never looked back to check if we were following—just kept skipping forward, turning left at a collapsed fence, then right past a pile of rubble that might have been a shop or a home.

After a few minutes, she stopped and pointed ahead, beaming.

"There! My house!" She pumped her fists in the air. "My house, my house!"

Even in the middle of all this—the destruction, the chaos, the fear—she'd found joy in the moment. What it is to be young.

We arrived at a home that had survived the hurricane with surprising strength. Two stories of heavy stone, walls the color of dusted granite, still standing despite the chaos around it. The rear roof had been torn away, beams exposed, dark voids showing the damage inside. Windows remained mostly intact, framed by rough-cut wood streaked with mud. Six solar panels, bent and cracked, lined the ground, their metal frames twisted, some edges flared, but still providing a faint trickle of power.

A small pen along the side, rebuilt with scrap wood, held three pigs and a handful of chickens. They were covered in dirt and mud but alive—proof of the care the family had taken during the storm. Flower beds had been battered, soil washed away, yet stubborn marigolds and hibiscus clung to life, gripping the cracked concrete around the foundation.

At the front, an elderly man and woman appeared. Smiles on their faces, lines in their skin deepened by age and hard work, they carried quiet confidence. The woman reached out, grip firm. She thanked us for coming, noting that no one else had made it this far. "You are the first."

Corey and I introduced ourselves. The couple did the same—the man was a local pastor named Jean-Claude, his wife Marie. She gripped my hand again, harder this time.

"You crossed the river," she said, eyes moving between us and the trucks. "No one else has crossed. How did you do it?"

"The people on the other side," I said. "They dug the bank down so we could climb it. Made it possible."

Jean-Claude shook his head slowly, something between disbelief and gratitude crossing his face. "They did this for you? In the dark? In the rain?"

"They did it for their village," Corey said. "For everyone who needs help."

Marie's eyes filled, but she didn't let the tears fall. "You are brave to come here. Foolish, maybe, but brave. God brought you."

I nodded.

"How many are you?" Jean-Claude asked, looking past us toward the trucks.

"Seven total," I said. "We have medical supplies, water filters, some food. Things for the kids. We'll do what we can."

Marie spoke softly but with conviction. "Our home is your home. There are three bedrooms upstairs. They are all yours. It is not much, but it is dry and safe."

"That's more than enough," I said. "Thank you."

Jean-Claude stepped closer, his voice quiet but firm. "Just being here, just coming when no one else would—that is already more than we could have hoped for. My people will be grateful."

Marie nodded. "I will tell them tonight. In the morning, they will come."

***

Corey returned to the trucks to brief the others. Gear was unloaded, introductions made, and the team headed upstairs to claim beds. I stayed behind, seated by the threshold, candlelight flickering over the rough stone.

I spoke quietly with the couple about the damage, urgent medical needs, and the work ahead. Plans were sketched, though sleep came first. She promised to alert the villagers, preparing them for the people who'd need care in the morning.

After about forty-five minutes, I headed upstairs where the others had settled in.

Upstairs, the rooms were modest but solid. Two to three beds per room, some people doubled up, most claiming a space for themselves. I slept on the floor next to a bed, letting the stone walls absorb the day's tension: the river crossing, the devastation, the endless effort of people just trying to survive. Outside, faint sounds filtered in—animals, distant water, the whisper of wind through the broken landscape. For the first time in hours, maybe days, my mind was clear.

The rain began to pour.

14

Infected Waters

I WOKE TO THE soft patter of small feet on the wooden floor. A little girl, no more than six or seven, stood above me, her eyes bright and curious. I offered a slow smile from my spot on the floor, still curled against the chill of the stone beneath me. She pressed a finger to her lips—Shhh—and then quietly whispered, "They are here."

Before I could ask who, she darted back down the stairs. I pushed myself up, rubbing the stiffness from my shoulders, and looked around the room. Most of the volunteers were still asleep, curled beneath thin blankets, breathing slow and steady. One of them, already awake, stood at the window, staring outside.

"You need to see this."

I walked over and looked. Outside, a line of people stretched down the dirt path—fifty, maybe sixty, waiting patiently. Some shifted from foot to foot. Others held infants. The sun was just rising, casting long shadows across the crowd. My throat tightened.

I turned to the room and gently woke everyone. "It's time. Time to go to work."

Clothes were thrown on, blankets folded. The small hallway became a swirl of movement as everyone shared the bathroom, brushing teeth and washing faces from small pails of clean water the children had brought up. There was no running water, no hot showers. Later, we'd figure that out. For now, this was enough.

Fifteen minutes later, everyone was ready. We gathered downstairs. Marie motioned toward a long wooden table, the rough grain worn smooth by years of use.

"Sit."

We hesitated. Outside, the line of people waited, quiet and patient.

"They will wait. It is important that you eat first. You will need the strength."

We sat. Soon, she'd placed a simple breakfast before us: bread, beans, sausage, and thick coffee, the aroma strong enough to chase away the morning chill.

No one said a word while eating. The silence felt unusual—not uncomfortable exactly, but noticeable. A few people glanced around the table, forks pausing mid-bite, as if trying to figure out if they'd missed some unspoken cue or broken a rule they didn't know existed.

Marie seemed to notice. She set down her cup and looked at us with a gentle smile.

"We eat in silence here. I hope it's not too uncomfortable for everyone."

She paused, letting the words settle.

"It's our way of showing appreciation—for the food's source, for the hands that prepared it, for the fact that we have it at all. In a place where so many have lost so much, gratitude shouldn't be rushed or buried under conversation. It should be felt. Honored."

Her voice was calm, unhurried. Not preachy. Just matter-of-fact, like she was explaining the way the sun rises.

"Silence lets us remember that not everyone woke up to a meal this morning. And it reminds us to be present—here, now—instead of already thinking about what comes next."

She picked up her cup again, took a sip, and gave a small nod.

"That's all. Just our way."

No one spoke after that, but the silence felt different. Intentional now. I found myself chewing slower, tasting the coffee, feeling the warmth of the bread in my hands. Around the table,

I saw others doing the same—present in the moment, grateful for it.

The warmth filled more than our stomachs. It steadied us. Gave us focus for what we were getting ready to do.

***

When the meal was finished, we stepped outside. A table had already been set up by some of the local kids, the surface scratched and weathered but solid. We unpacked the medical gear, sorting supplies with methodical precision. Everyone found their place. Roles fell naturally into order.

And then, with nothing more than a glance at one another, we began.

We worked without pause for the next seven hours. The line never thinned. Some injuries were minor—scrapes, cuts, infections. Others were severe: jagged lacerations, eyes clouded with dirt and tiny metal fragments, wounds punched open by rebar or debris hurled in the hurricane's fury.

We set up stations along the tables, dividing tasks as efficiently as possible. One table cleaned and dressed wounds. Another stabilized fractures. Others monitored fevers and handed out water and pain relief. Mercius moved with quiet authority, speaking to people in rapid French, explaining treatments, calming fears, making the process less terrifying. The volunteers, some new to work like this, found their rhythm quickly.

The sun climbed higher. The courtyard turned into a furnace. Heat and humidity made every movement harder, every breath thick with dust and antiseptic. Sweat stung my eyes. My shirt stuck to my back. My hands started blistering from scrubbing and gripping tools for hours.

But no one stopped. We were here because we wanted to be.

Every person who came forward carried evidence of the storm's force. Broken ribs. Lacerations. Infections that could have killed within days if left untreated. We stitched, we cleaned, we wrapped, we stabilized.

Children huddled at the edges of the courtyard, some hiding behind parents, others watching intently. Their small hands clutched scraps of clothing or corners of blankets. Every so often, one would be called forward, a minor injury cleaned and bandaged, and their wide eyes would flicker with gratitude or fear, sometimes both at once.

Hours passed, unmarked except by the rising sun and the slow exhaustion creeping into our muscles. By mid-afternoon, the heat had become nearly unbearable. The smell of sweat, dust, and antiseptic in the air.

***

That afternoon a woman approached. She moved with purpose, her face tight with worry. She pulled me aside, Mercius close behind. In rapid French, she spoke to him. Mercius listened, occasionally nodding, his brow furrowed. Minutes passed. When he finally looked back at me, his expression had changed.

"She says many people up the road are suddenly getting sick. She fears a disease is spreading. She needs help—immediately."

I nodded, already thinking ahead. "I'll gather a few volunteers and some basic medical supplies. We'll head up the road, treat who we can, and find the source."

Three of us moved quickly, leaving the house behind. The road twisted and climbed, flanked by shattered trees and flattened crops, debris scattered everywhere. After roughly twenty minutes, we arrived at another small village, its residents waiting anxiously.

The woman who'd come to us was there, along with several others. She explained the situation again, her voice shaking, hands gesturing toward a cluster of makeshift shelters where the sick lay on mats and blankets.

We moved through the group, checking symptoms. Fever. Vomiting. Diarrhea. Severe dehydration in some of the children. The pattern was consistent—classic signs of water-borne illness. But determining the exact pathogen without lab equipment was impossible. We could treat the symptoms, rehydrate them, give them antibiotics, but if the source wasn't eliminated, more people would get sick.

I started asking questions through Mercius. Where do you get your water? A nearby stream, they said. Do you boil it? Sometimes. Not always. How many people are sick? Fifteen so far. More complaining of stomach pain.

I pulled Mercius aside. "They're all drinking from the same source. That's the connection. But something's contaminating it. It has to be upstream."

He nodded. "We need to find it."

I looked at the volunteers with me. "We're going to have to hike the stream. Follow it up, and if we're lucky we will find the source of the problem."

One of them—a young woman who'd been mostly quiet up until now—spoke up. "What if it's a long way?"

"Then we walk a long way." I smiled. Not worried—certain.

We left basic supplies with the village—oral rehydration salts, clean water we'd brought, instructions to boil everything.

One of the healthier villagers agreed to help distribute the salts and make sure people understood the dosing. It wasn't a permanent solution, but it would buy time.

The three of us regrouped at the edge of the village. We divided what we'd need—flashlights, water bottles, a basic first aid kit in case we ran into trouble. The stream ran along the base of the hill, disappearing into dense brush and broken trees about a hundred yards up.

Mercius pointed. "It goes that way. Through there."

I looked at the terrain. Thick undergrowth. Mud. Debris everywhere. It wasn't going to be a quick hike.

"Alright. Let's move."

We turned upstream and started walking.

We hiked along the river, through mud, under low-hanging branches, past twisted metal and shattered wood. Hours stretched. The sun lowered. Shadows thickened. Sweat dripped into eyes stinging from dust.

Just as the frustration began to settle in, a volunteer standing on a small rise shouted. "Here! I found something!"

We scrambled up to him, peering down at the water below. Amid the debris—branches, uprooted plants, drifting scraps—we saw forms, barely distinguishable in the churning reflection.

Carefully, we descended toward the riverbank, boots sinking in mud, hands brushing against reeds and rocks for balance. The closer we got, the clearer it became.

Floating in the water were several dead horses, bloated and drifting, their eyes clouded, bodies swaying with the current. Two human corpses bobbed nearby, their forms twisted in decay, partially hidden beneath waterlogged debris. The stench hit instantly—thick, coppery, mixed with the river's mud, overpowering everything.

This was the source. The contamination that had sickened the village originated here, upstream.

I crouched at the edge, hands on my knees, staring at the water. We needed to act quickly. The volunteers around me moved silently, each taking in the scene, each preparing for the next steps: containment, cleanup, triage.

I made the decision to pull everything from the water—the horses, the bodies—lifting them high enough onto the shore so they no longer tainted the river. It was grim work, but necessary. The water was the lifeblood of the villages downstream. Once we finished, we'd head back, relay our findings, and organize for able-bodied villagers to return and properly bury the dead. That way, families could identify them if they recognized someone missing. A small measure of closure.

It took over an hour to get everything out of the water. The work was physically exhausting, but the mental strain was something else entirely. There was a disconnect in lifting decaying bodies with hands that moments before were checking for pulse, treating cuts, reassuring frightened villagers. How do you honor the dead in a moment like that? How do you stay human while moving corpses with the same determination you use to protect the living? There was no time to think about it. You just had to find a balance between efficiency and respect to get the job done.

The sun climbed higher. The heat pressed down, mixing with the stench of river and decay. Sweat ran into eyes. Clothes clung with mud and water. But we kept at it. Each body, each animal, lifted with the same careful, methodical motion. A silent acknowledgment of the life that had been and the living that depended on our work.

***

We arrived back at the house just after sunset. The volunteers had wrapped up their work maybe half an hour before, and the entire place felt transformed.

Children were everywhere. Dozens of them. Their laughter carried across the yard. One of the volunteers had somehow hauled a small projector in her pack, and she'd rigged it to throw a Disney movie across the whitewashed wall of the house. The picture flickered and wobbled in the evening breeze, but the kids didn't care. They sat shoulder to shoulder, wide-eyed, some with their chins resting on their knees.

The rest darted around the yard in games only children could invent—hide-and-seek around broken trees, tag through the dust, little dramas where sticks became swords and someone always had to be the dragon. Another volunteer sat cross-legged in the dirt with a circle of kids around her, showing them how to fold paper into birds. Their concentration was fierce and earnest.

For a moment, everything the day had thrown at us—the injuries, the fear in people's eyes, the bodies in the river—slipped to the edges of my mind long enough for me to take a full breath. Not forget. Just breathe.

There was something good in the scene. Something simple. The kind of goodness that didn't need to be loud or praised or pretend the world wasn't broken. It just existed anyway—quiet, stubborn, real.

As exhausted as I was, as dirty and sunburned and over-heated as we all were, standing there watching those kids felt like a reminder of why we'd come. Not for glory or acknowl-edgement. Not for stories. But for this—tiny pockets of life returning where death had spent the morning.

Human beings caring for each other. Laughing again. Feel-ing safe again. Belonging to one another the way we're sup-posed to.

That small, ordinary thing was enough to close the day. Enough to make every hard thing worth it. And as the night settled over the village, I realized something I hadn't under-stood the day before:

Not all rescue work is tragedy. Some of it is bringing things back to life.

15

Lima Charlie

B Y MID-MORNING OF THE second day, we were drowning. The line had doubled overnight—people walking from villages we hadn't even heard of yet. We'd already treated fifty, maybe sixty. And we were running out of supplies.

I wiped my hands on my pants and stepped away from the table. The pastor appeared at my side, his face drawn, eyes red from too little sleep.

"There are more coming," he said quietly. "Farther villages. Many have not eaten. Many injuries are worsening."

I nodded. "We're close to the edge. We can stretch what we have, but not for long."

He understood. So did the volunteers who overheard.

I pulled out my satellite phone and moved to a quiet corner outside the house. A few rings later, Becca answered.

"How are you guys doing? I didn't hear from you yesterday—I was starting to worry."

"We reached a place in desperate need. Crossing a river that no one else could manage, we got through safely. Yesterday, we treated over a hundred people."

I could hear her inhale sharply.

"But here's the problem—we're running out of everything. By the end of the day, food, medical supplies... all of it will be gone."

There was a pause, then her tone shifted, measured but determined. "Okay. I can handle this. I'll reach out to a few people I've been working with in back channels—others who are in the area. Maybe someone can help. But... is there a way for them to get in?"

"Not right now. Crossing the river would be dangerous. Rushing water, unpredictable depth. But if you can find someone to bring supplies to a point on the other side, we can figure out a way to move them across safely."

"Okay."

We finished confirming the details, and I ended the call. Standing in the corner, I watched the sunlight shift across the stone walls. The village was alive with activity, the hum rising with each passing minute.

For a moment I watched a small, elderly man mixing mud and clay, packing it into small wooden square molds he'd made. Baking them in the sunshine. Making bricks.

None of it was guaranteed. None of it came easily. But somehow, the moment—the people, the work, the possibility of connection—was enough.

I squared my shoulders and moved back to my station, working through the line. For a few hours, it was steady—cleaning, flushing, bandaging. Then a boy, maybe fourteen, stood in front of me. Eyes wide, he hesitated.

"Hey, what's going on?"

"My grandmother... she needs help." He turned, pointing to an elderly woman seated on a low concrete wall a short distance away, her back hunched.

"Can she walk?"

"Yes... strong woman. We made it this far."

"How far?"

He pointed toward the mountains beyond the river. "From there."

I swallowed hard, imagining their journey. I stood and walked with him toward her. Kneeling, I looked into her eyes. Life had carved lines into her face. Her gaze held wisdom—and pain too deep for words.

"Let's get you to the table."

She rose slowly. I took her arm, the boy took the other. Each step careful, and deliberate.

Once seated, I scanned her face, neck, arms, legs. Nothing appeared unusual at first.

"What's wrong?"

"Her chest." He pointed.

"Heart condition?"

"No, it's open," he said.

I was confused. Open? "Can I see her?"

He whispered something in Creole, and she carefully lifted her dress. My stomach clenched. The wound was roughly the size of a fist, deep, ragged and wide open. How she had survived this long, I couldn't fathom.

"This... this is bad." I wanted to fix it, but we didn't have the supplies. She needed a hospital—fast.

The boy's eyes searched mine. "She... survive?"

"I don't know. We need to get her help. Fast."

I stood, pacing for a moment. "Keep her here." I turned to a nearby volunteer, who had seen the wound. Her eyes were wide. "Give her water, food... anything she needs. Don't leave her alone. I'll be back in a few minutes."

"I won't."

I glanced back at the boy. "Stay with her. I'll be back."

"Yes. Ok." He gripped her hand.

I moved away from the table, mind racing. I pulled out my satellite phone again and dialed Becca. She answered immediately.

"I have a bad one, Bec. I need a hospital."

"Hold on." The sound of rapid typing in the background. After a few seconds, she was back on the line.

"I've got you help. I've been working on it all morning."

"Tell me what I need to do to make it happen."

"I need your longitude and latitude. The local U.S. military base has agreed to drop one round of supplies—medical, food, clothing. They're loading them now."

I could barely believe it. Timing like this was impossible to plan, yet somehow it felt inevitable.

I paused, thinking of the woman in front of me. "Will they take her? The one who needs urgent care?"

There was a short silence. "I don't know."

I exhaled slowly. "Then I'm going to have to talk them into it myself."

She chuckled softly. "I figured you might."

We finished confirming the details for the supply drop. I ended the call and immediately went to find Corey, who was kneeling beside the small water filtration system, setting it up.

"Supplies are on their way. They're being airlifted in, but we need to clear a landing zone first. Fifty yards by fifty yards. All debris removed—nothing can get caught in the rotor wash."

He straightened, eyes widening. "And what are they flying in?"

"Everything we need."

"Except a hospital." A half-smile hiding what he meant.

"Except a hospital."

He scanned the surrounding terrain, already making mental notes. "Got it. We can clear a path."

I glanced back toward the woman, her grandson still holding her hand. The urgency of the supply drop was incredible, yes, but nothing could overshadow the immediate need right here. The sick, the injured, the ones we could reach right now—they were our first priority.

I returned to the woman and worked quickly to create a small space away from the others. I cleaned the laceration as best I could, flushing out debris and packing it firmly with gauze. Every movement had to be careful; one wrong shift could worsen the wound. Her grandson hovered close, silent, gripping her hand like as if it was then last time.

Meanwhile, Corey rallied a few of the locals to clear a safe landing zone. I turned to the pastor and asked for four of his strongest men to manage security. They would keep everyone away from the aircraft, ensure no one interfered, and help move the supplies to a secure location once the drop was complete. Without hesitation, he sprang into action.

An hour and a half later, a distant roar cut through the afternoon air. The V-22 Osprey was overhead, the whip of its blades slicing through the tension. It circled the clearing several times, tracking every movement, every branch, every piece of debris. Corey had done his job well; the landing zone was clean and ready.

A little past three, the Osprey touched down. The ramp dropped, and supplies waited inside. We started a chain, hands moving quickly, unloading food, medical gear, and boxes of clothing as if each crate carried the promise of life itself.

I pulled the pilot aside. "There's someone who needs immediate care or she's not going to make it."

He shook his head. "No can do."

But then he paused, thought for a moment, and stepped back into the aircraft. I watched as he picked up a small radio, speaking rapidly. His eyes flicked to me several times. Moments later, he returned, breathing hard.

"Keep this LZ clear. I called in a favor to a friend who runs a small medevac team in PAP. He's en route now and agreed to lift your wounded."

I didn't need to say anything. Relief hit me like a wave, sharp and raw. The woman would get help.

"Thank you." I gripped his hand.

He nodded once. "Anytime."

The pilot jogged back to the Osprey, gave quick instructions to his crew, and within minutes they'd finished unloading. The ramp closed, the engines roared, and the aircraft lifted off, banking hard to the west before disappearing over the hills.

We moved the supplies to a covered area near the house—stacks of boxes, crates of medical gear, bags of rice and beans. The volunteers worked fast, organizing everything by category while the pastor's men stood guard. Meanwhile, I returned to the woman and her grandson.

She was resting, eyes half-closed, breathing shallow but steady. The wound was packed as well as I could manage, but it wasn't enough. Not nearly enough. Her grandson sat beside her, one hand on her arm, watching her face like he was afraid she'd disappear if he looked away.

"She's stable for now," I told him. "Help is coming."

He nodded, but didn't speak. Just kept watching her. I'm not sure if he believed me in that moment.

I checked my watch. Thirty minutes, the pilot had said. Maybe less.

The waiting felt longer than it should have. I kept working—cleaning wounds, distributing water, checking fevers—but my attention kept drifting back to her. Every few minutes, I'd glance over, making sure she was still breathing, still holding on.

Then, faint at first, I heard it. The distant thump of rotor blades.

I looked up. The medevac helicopter came in low over the trees, circling once to assess the landing zone before descending. Its blades whipped the dust and debris into small storms around us. The moment it touched down, the side door slid open. Aside from the pilot, three physicians clambered out, moving quickly. They joined us immediately, checking patients, stabilizing injuries, lending hands and expertise where it was needed most.

I stayed close to the woman and her grandson as they worked, feeling the tension in her small frame slowly ease with each measured movement of the doctors. Then, after thirty minutes of careful attention, they lifted her onto a stretcher. Her grandson clutched her hand one last time. I could see the worry still etched in his young face, but also a flicker of hope.

They loaded both of them into the helicopter, waved briefly, and then the aircraft rose, blades screaming against the dying light of the day. The dust settled slowly, the roar faded, and quiet descended over the camp.

I stood there for a long moment, taking in the scene—the cleared landing zone, the remaining supplies, the exhausted but steady volunteers moving among the people. The day had been brutal, but now it held something rare.

So often, these days ended with exhaustion and frustration, with lives hanging in the balance and no way to fix it all. But today, the impossible had happened.

I exhaled. The tension I'd been carrying all day finally eased.

We'd won this one. Not every time. Not most of the time. But today, we had.

The grandmother was safe. The supplies had arrived. The village had what it needed to make it through another few days.

For now, that was enough.

16

The Request

I SAT UP ON the patch of dirt I had claimed behind the house. I must have wanted the stars, the quiet air. Somewhere in that intent, I had drifted off. My back ached, stiff and sore.

The air was already clinging, a promise of another day that would test every ounce of strength we had. I pulled my hat down, wiped sleep from my eyes, and stepped around to the front of the house.

The camp had already woken without me. People moved like a single organism, tending wounds, distributing the scraps of food and supplies left.

I exhaled, long, steady. No time to wake up. The day had already begun.

Corey appeared, stretching his arms, rolling his shoulders, the lines of exhaustion still etched into his face. But there was something else there too—relief, maybe. Hope.

"You get any sleep?"

"About as much as you did." I smirked.

Corey chuckled. "So... none, then."

I nodded toward the camp. "Everyone's already in place, working away."

"Yeah. What we've done here... this? It's good."

I looked at the people. I could see the change—something that felt like hope, fragile but there.

"Yeah. It is. It definitely is."

Corey clapped me on the back once, firm. "A point for the team."

We were heading toward the clinic when a low rumble drifted in from down the road. At first it was faint—just another vibration in a place full of them—but then it grew, layered, mechanical. Not the distant thud of a generator or the muffled churn of a pump. This was movement. A lot of it.

Corey stopped mid-stride. "You hear that?"

Before I could answer, dust lifted beyond the trees. Children froze mid-play. Adults paused with bandages and buckets in hand. The road began to spit up a long, pale plume.

Two trucks rounded the bend, heavy, engines straining under the weight of whatever they were carrying. They rolled to a stop in front of the house, brakes hissing. Doors swung open and several people climbed out.

I stepped forward to meet them.

A woman broke off from the small group and came toward me, brushing dust from her shirt, her expression bright despite everything.

"We heard you were doing good work here. A lot of people have heard. Kind of big news."

"We're doing our best."

She glanced back toward the road. "The river dropped overnight. Not by much, but enough. Crossing wasn't a problem this morning."

"That's good. You made it. Welcome."

She looked at me for a second, like maybe she'd expected something more. But we weren't here for headlines. We were here to help people.

She nodded, her face shifting into something more serious—purpose settling in behind her eyes. "We brought supplies."

They were volunteers from another organization, dusty from the road and carrying the same worn look of those who had seen too much and kept moving anyway. Word had reached them about our camp, about the river crossing, about the chaos we were somehow managing to hold together. Now they were here, boots sinking into the soft soil as they stepped out of the trucks, taking in the scene with quick, assessing eyes.

The woman who'd spoken first introduced herself as Claire. French-Canadian, spoke three languages, had been doing relief work in Haiti for six years. Behind her came the others—a Haitian nurse named Josette, two American paramedics who looked like they were barely out of college, a mechanic from Gonaïves named René, and a midwife from Port-de-Paix whose name I didn't catch at first but later learned was Nadège.

They moved with the efficiency of people who'd done this before. No wasted motion. No hesitation. Within minutes, they'd formed a chain from the truck beds to the house, passing boxes hand to hand like a well-rehearsed dance.

Medical kits. Sacks of rice. Water purifiers. Boxes of clothing. Diapers. Tarps. And then, near the end, something unexpected—toys. Stuffed animals, dolls, soccer balls, coloring books. One of the paramedics caught my eye as he passed a box labeled "KIDS" in thick black marker.

"Figured they could use something normal," he said.

I nodded. That was smart. The kids needed something beyond bandages and fear.

The unloading took maybe an hour, but the mood shifted almost immediately. The supplies were plenty now. No longer a worry of running out. And more than that—the arrival of these people, strangers who'd driven through uncertain roads just to help, felt like proof that the work mattered. That people cared.

One of the volunteers—a young woman with a shaved head and tired eyes—sat down near the makeshift clinic and started organizing medical supplies with Marie. They worked quietly at first, sorting gauze and antibiotics, but then Marie said something in Creole that made the woman laugh. A real laugh, the kind that breaks tension. Soon they were trading stories—Marie about her children, the woman about losing her own home in the last storm season and deciding that if she couldn't rebuild her place, she might as well help someone else rebuild theirs.

Nearby, René the mechanic had already pulled Corey aside and was inspecting our water filtration setup. Within minutes, he'd spotted a loose connection and tightened it with a wrench he'd pulled from his pocket. "This would've failed in a day," he said matter-of-factly. Corey grinned. "Good thing you showed up."

The midwife, Nadège, moved through the crowd with a calm authority that reminded me of Marie. She stopped to check on a pregnant woman who'd been sitting in the shade all morning, spoke to her softly in Creole, then called over one of our volunteers to bring water and fruit. She didn't make a big deal of it. Just did what needed doing.

***

By mid-afternoon, the children had discovered the toys. A group of them descended on the boxes, shrieking with delight as they pulled out stuffed animals and balls. One little girl found a doll with braided hair and clutched it to her chest like it was made of gold. A boy, maybe ten, grabbed a soccer ball and immediately started organizing a game in the clearing.

Mercius saw the ball and his face lit up. He jogged over, said something in Creole that made the boys laugh, and within seconds he was in the middle of the game, barefoot in the dirt, moving with the easy grace of someone who'd grown up playing in streets just like this one.

I watched from the clinic as he weaved through the pack of kids, all of them shouting and laughing. He faked left, the boys lunged, and he slipped the ball past them into a makeshift goal—two sticks someone had jammed into the ground. The kids erupted. Mercius threw his hands in the air, grinning wide, and for the first time since we'd arrived, he looked like a teenager instead of someone carrying the pressure of the world.

One of the American paramedics—a guy named Josh—walked over and stood beside me, watching the game.

"That kid's got moves."

"Yeah. He does."

Josh smiled. "Good to see him smiling. Good to see any of them smiling."

I nodded. It was.

***

Around four in the afternoon, someone started a fire in the center of the compound. I'm not sure who. By the time I noticed, there was already a ring of people gathering around it—volunteers, villagers, children. The pastor brought out a pot of something that smelled incredible. Rice and beans, cooked slow with spices I couldn't name. Marie appeared with bread, still warm.

People sat in the dirt, passing bowls, eating with their hands or whatever utensils they could find. The conversation was a mix of Creole, French, and English, voices overlapping, laughter rising and falling. One of the volunteers—Claire—told a story about getting her truck stuck in mud up to the axles and having to be pulled out by a farmer with an ox. The way she told it, with exaggerated gestures and mock outrage, had everyone doubled over.

Nadège, the midwife, countered with a story about delivering a baby during a blackout with nothing but a headlamp and sheer stubbornness. "The baby came out screaming," she said. "I told the mother, 'He's already angry at the world. He'll do fine.'" More laughter.

Even the pastor smiled, a rare sight. He sat with his wife, their shoulders touching, watching the fire and the people around it with quiet satisfaction.

I found myself sitting next to Josette, the Haitian nurse. She was older, maybe in her fifties, with kind eyes and hands that never stopped moving—always reaching for something, adjusting something, helping someone.

"You've been doing this a long time," I said.

She nodded. "Twenty years. Maybe more. I lose track."

"Why?"

She looked at me like the question was strange. "Because people need help. What else would I do?"

It wasn't rhetorical. She genuinely didn't understand the alternative.

"You have family?" I asked.

"Three daughters. All grown now. One's a teacher. One's a nurse like me. The youngest is still in school." She smiled. "They think I'm crazy for doing this. But they understand."

"Do they?"

"They help when they can. My middle daughter—she's the one who convinced this group to come. She saw a post online about your camp. Showed it to Claire. And here we are."

I looked around the fire, at the faces lit by the glow. Strangers an hour ago. Now something closer to family.

"Tell her thank you," I said.

Josette smiled. "I will."

As the sun dropped below the hills, the soccer game finally ended. The kids collapsed in the grass, panting and grinning, too tired to keep going. Mercius jogged over to the fire, drenched in sweat, and someone handed him water. He drank it in one long pull, then dropped down next to one of the boys and started teaching him some kind of hand-clapping game. The boy struggled at first, missing the rhythm, but Mercius just laughed and slowed it down until the kid got it. Then they were both clapping and laughing, and other kids crowded around to watch.

Corey sat across the fire from me, talking to René about engine repair. I caught his eye and he gave me a small nod. The kind that said, *This is good. We did good.*

And we had.

For the first time in days, the camp didn't feel like a crisis. It felt like a community. People helping people. Sharing food. Telling stories. Laughing.

It felt human.

Later, as the fire settled into a soft orange bed of coals, the pastor came over. He waited for the conversation to quiet, then spoke with the kind of careful calm that tells you the news isn't good.

He explained that a supply route—about an hour from us—had been compromised. Several of his church members had reported it earlier that day. With the river finally receding enough to make the crossing manageable, he thought we might be able to help.

I listened as he laid it out. A gang had taken control of a narrow choke point in the road. They waited for aid vehicles, forced them to stop, and stripped them at gunpoint—food, fuel, medicine—gone before any of it reached the villages on the other side.

He looked at Corey, then at me.

"They want to try again tomorrow. Would you be willing to help?"

The fire cracked between us. No one rushed to answer.

The question sat there. Unanswered.

The past twenty-four hours played through my mind—the woman lifted out by medevac, the Osprey settling into the clearing, the strangers who arrived with trucks full of supplies. Every one of those moments had come because someone stepped forward when it would've been easier not to.

I lifted my head and met the pastor's stare. "Yeah. We'll take a swing at it."

Corey looked over, caught my eye, and nodded. A faint smile crossed the pastor's face—not excitement, just relief that someone was willing to step into the gap again.

The night pressed in around us, warm and thick, carrying the faint smell of diesel from the trucks parked in a loose half-circle near the house. The new volunteers sat in small clusters, swapping stories in low voices, their sentences drifting in and out of Creole and English.

For a moment I drifted back to a memory from when I was a kid—standing with my father at the corner of a neighborhood street after a bad storm. Power lines down, sirens in the distance, a crowd forming around an intersection blocked by a fallen tree. My father didn't say much. He never did. But he looked at me, then at the people waiting, then back at the tree. "If you can help, you help. That's the whole thing. Everything else is noise." And then he climbed over the trunk and started clearing branches, no audience, no hesitation.

That simplicity had stuck with me. It had become its own kind of compass.

I felt it now.

Corey stepped up beside me, handed me a cup of water, and stayed quiet. He didn't need an explanation. Leadership had snuck up on us both in the same way. One day we were simply two guys who'd shown up; now people waited for us to speak before they made their own decisions. Not out of hierarchy. Out of trust. That's a heavier thing.

"Tomorrow's going to be long."

"Yeah."

He nodded once, the way he always does when he's already accepted the hard part.

We stayed by the fire until it was nothing but a dull red glow then headed for our racks.

17

Choke Point

COREY AND I WALKED through the shattered village in the early morning light. I thought about suffering. Not just ours, not just theirs, but the constant presence of it everywhere. The Buddhists say life is pain. Illness, loss, desire, death—they're inseparable from living. The wisdom isn't in denying suffering, but in meeting it with awareness.

Humility comes first—recognizing how small our own problems are against the vastness of hardship around us. Gratitude follows—for survival, for the chance to act. Beyond that comes action: love and compassion extended outward, to all people. The practice is deliberate, and it costs something. To see the world clearly and still choose generosity isn't easy—but it's necessary.

I turned to Corey. "Time to move."

He nodded.

The pastor met us at the front of his home.

"Good morning. Today is the day."

"Yes. Today is the day."

"There are three trucks loaded with supplies waiting on the other side of the river. My wife and I packed some lunches for you—we hope you enjoy them." He handed us a paper sack. "Inside is one for Mercius as well. May God bless your day... and good luck getting through. Our entire congregation is praying for you."

I smiled. It was a nice thing to hear. "Thank you. We'll do our best."

Mercius walked up, ready to go. I handed him a paper sack. "Here—your lunch."

He looked inside briefly, then smiled. Corey chuckled beside me.

We loaded essentials into the truck: radios, water, a small medical kit, and the lunches. Over the past few days, people in the community had started helping clean things up. The roads were first. It was good to see them cleared, making travel easier.

We reached the river. The water had receded significantly. It was still high, but the current had slowed enough to give us confidence. We inched forward, tires crunching over shifting stones, and made it to the other side without incident.

Three trucks waited, engines idling, drivers alert. I pulled alongside them. Corey handed Mercius a radio for each truck.

"Each driver gets one. We'll go first. They follow. Once we reach the choke point, they fall back until we're through, then we radio them to move. If we get pinned, they turn back immediately—no questions."

Mercius explained everything in French. One of the men ran between the trucks, handing out radios. When he climbed back in, he gave us a thumbs-up.

We were off.

The dirt road stretched ahead, narrow and uneven, lined with dense trees. Tires bounced over rocks, dust rising behind us. Mercius called out landmarks quietly. Corey mapped the route on a small tablet.

We drove in silence, the kind that comes when everyone knows the stakes. I kept scanning for movement in the treeline, for shadows that didn't belong.

"You've done this before?" I asked Mercius quietly.

"No, but I trust you and Corey. I don't trust many people. The rebels—they know the road. They wait. They choose carefully. I know you'll choose carefully too."

Every convoy was a gamble. Every attempt before ours had ended with emptied trucks and broken spirits.

I tightened my grip on the steering wheel. This wasn't a race. It was patience, precision, and nerves made of steel.

And then, just ahead, the first bend that led into the ambush point came into view.

We'd planned for this. Before leaving the village, I'd pulled the team together and walked through the likely scenarios. Checkpoint. Ambush. Robbery. Each had a protocol.

"If we hit resistance," I'd said, "we don't scatter. We don't improvise. One person talks. Everyone else stays visible, hands clear, no sudden moves. The other trucks stay back—quarter mile minimum—until we signal all-clear."

Corey had nodded. "And if they want the supplies?"

"We stall. We negotiate. We don't fight. These trucks aren't worth dying over."

Now, creeping along the narrow road with two trucks trailing at exactly a quarter-mile, I saw it: a tree dragged across the path. The choke point.

I keyed the radio. "Hold position. Eyes up."

The trucks behind us stopped. Engines stayed running.

I slowed our truck, hands visible on the wheel, eyes scanning the treeline. And then they appeared.

Rebels slipped out from either side. Not soldiers. Just boys, mostly. Teenagers with old rifles. Their clothes were torn, faded, caked with dust. One wore a Manchester United jersey. But their eyes were hard. Old. The kind you get when hunger and fear become routine.

Eight, maybe ten of them. They moved with practiced efficiency, rifles raised.

My heart hammered. Adrenaline lit every nerve. But I kept my hands on the wheel. Protocol.

Mercius stepped from the truck first, hands open—exactly as we'd discussed. Corey followed, slow and deliberate, hands slightly raised. I stayed behind the wheel. If anyone was going to take the first hit, it would be us. That was the plan.

The leader stepped forward. Couldn't have been more than nineteen. Thin, wiry, a scar running from his ear to his jaw. His rifle was an old AK, the stock wrapped in duct tape.

He barked something in Creole. The others tightened their circle. Gun barrels waved.

The standoff stretched. The leader spoke again, louder. Mercius responded, voice calm. Back and forth. Rapid Creole I couldn't follow.

I watched the other rebels while Mercius negotiated. Most of them were scared. You could see it in how they held the rifles—too tight, fingers twitching. One kid, maybe fifteen, kept glancing back at the trees like he wanted to run.

They weren't hardened fighters. They were desperate. That gave us leverage.

Mercius leaned back toward the truck. "He wants everything. All three trucks. Says if we don't give them, they take them anyway."

I'd anticipated this. Before we left, I'd considered what we had that they didn't: reach. Connection. The appearance of power.

I kept my eyes on the rifles and spoke into the radio, low and even. "Tell him if I key this twice, everything here disappears. Within minutes. Air support. Death from above."

Then I raised the radio high above my head, arm locked, thumb hovering over the transmit button.

It was a bluff. Complete bluff. But I sold it like I'd done it a hundred times before—calm, controlled, certain.

Mercius went still. His eyes flicked to mine, reading the play instantly. Then he relayed it word for word, his tone steady, authoritative.

The leader stared at the radio. Then at me. His jaw tightened. Nobody moved.

Then Corey spoke. Quiet, but firm. A few words in broken French. He pointed at the radio, then at the sky, then back at the leader.

The leader's posture changed. Just slightly.

Slowly, the barrels dipped. Not surrender. Not trust. Just a temporary choice to let the day move forward.

I lowered the radio but kept it visible.

"Are they stealing the transports?"

Mercius translated. The leader answered, shorter this time. Less aggressive.

"They have families. No one will help them. They don't want to see their families die."

I let that settle.

"We have three trucks full of supplies. They can take one. And every four days, I will personally make sure another arrives for them and their families. But only if they guarantee they won't threaten, harm, or take anything from us or anyone else again."

Mercius translated. The leader dropped his gaze, staring at the dirt. When he looked back at me, something shifted. Not weakness. Something simpler. Relief.

Relief that someone finally understood the cost of survival.

He spoke to Mercius. Mercius nodded, then turned to me.

"He agrees. They'll take the third truck. They won't stop you again."

"Tell him I'll keep my word. Every fourth day. But if they break theirs, the deal ends."

Mercius translated. The leader nodded once, sharp and certain.

Then he turned and spoke to his men. They lowered their rifles, stepped back.

Compassion alone doesn't resolve conflict. But compassion paired with resolve often opens a door.

The rebels helped unload the third truck. When it was empty, the leader shook Mercius's hand, then Corey's, then mine. His grip was firm.

He said something in Creole. Mercius translated. "He says thank you. And he's sorry."

I nodded. "Tell him we'll be back in two days."

We climbed back into the truck and continued down the road.

***

We reached the village just as the last light bled out of the sky. People were waiting. A few families, standing near the road, watching.

When we started unloading, they moved forward slowly, cautiously.

An older woman approached me. She took my hand in both of hers and held it. Her eyes were wet. She said something in Creole.

Mercius translated. "She says her grandchildren will eat tonight. Because of you."

I nodded.

We unloaded everything. The families helped, passing boxes hand to hand, their movements careful, reverent almost.

One of the men shook my hand, then Corey's. He spoke in broken English. "You come back?"

"Yes. We'll come back."

He smiled. "Good. We wait for you."

***

Over the next week, we kept the promise. Every fourth day, a truck arrived for the rebels. And every other day, we delivered supplies to villages that hadn't seen help in months.

We provided medical care to more than 400 people. We handed out over five tons of food. We rebuilt more than a dozen homes—including the pastors church and a primary school.

One afternoon, I watched Corey clean and dress a wound on a boy's arm. When he finished, the boy said something in Creole. Mercius smiled.

"He says you have gentle hands. Like his mother."

Corey's face softened. He paused, searching for the right words. "Tell him his mother raised him well."

The boy grinned. We all laughed.

By the end of our time there, I thought about what we'd done. Not the numbers. Not the supplies or the homes.

I thought about the woman who held my hand. The man who asked if we'd come back.

Suffering is constant. It's inevitable. Life will always test you and demand a choice.

What mattered was not the danger, not the chaos, but how we responded. Humility, gratitude, compassion—these weren't abstract ideals. They were actions, deliberate and cost-ly, carried out under sun and dust and the threat of violence.

We had ventured into that chaos armed with little more than intention, discipline, and the knowledge that love and care were sometimes the only shields we had. And somehow, by choosing to act, by choosing generosity over fear, we had found a thread of grace in the middle of suffering—a reminder that even in the darkest places, the human spirit can leave a mark that lasts longer than fear.

18

Survival Profile

OVER THE NEXT FEW years, the calls kept coming. Earthquakes. Hurricanes. Civil unrest. Villages erased by mud, by water, by fire. Each operation sharpened the skills, tested the limits, added another layer to what we carried.

I'd learned to move between disasters and conflict zones, but the human mind carries its own geography. Even when you cross borders, it doesn't shift nearly as fast.

By then, I no longer came home carrying the shock of a single event. I carried accumulation. Haiti became one chapter in a long list. Not forgotten, not minimized, but part of a broader pattern of human fragility.

Reintegration wasn't something I stumbled through anymore. It was a discipline. I knew the states I'd cycle through—fragmented sleep, sharpened reactions, thinning patience. I knew what it felt like to go from constant adrenaline to suburban silence. And I'd learned to navigate it.

I'd done this dozens of times. Deploy, return, adjust, deploy again. Each cycle taught me something the previous one hadn't. And after enough repetitions, a pattern emerged that challenged what I'd been told about trauma.

Most service members deploy once, maybe twice, then come home for good. When they struggle to reintegrate—when they can't sleep, can't sit still, can't find meaning in civilian routines—we call it PTSD. We treat it as damage. Permanent scarring from what they witnessed.

But I wasn't so sure.

What if it wasn't damage at all? What if it was transition?

I'd watched myself go through the same symptoms every time I came back. The hyper-vigilance. The restlessness. The way normal conversations felt hollow. The first time, I thought something was wrong with me. The second time, I recognized it. By the tenth time, I understood: this wasn't breaking. This was adjusting.

Your nervous system doesn't flip a switch. It recalibrates. When you've spent weeks operating in environments where awareness keeps you alive, where every sound matters, where hesitation kills—you can't just turn that off because you're back in a grocery store parking lot. Your body needs time to learn it's safe again. Your mind needs time to reorient.

The problem isn't the transition itself. It's that most people only do it once. They go from war zone to suburb in 48 hours, and then they're expected to stay in the suburb forever. Their nervous system is screaming that something's wrong, and everyone around them confirms it by calling it a disorder.

I had an advantage most didn't: I kept going back. Deploy, return, adjust, repeat. Each time, I learned the rhythm. I knew the crash would come, but I also knew it would pass. I knew the numbness wasn't permanent. I knew the hyper-vigilance would fade as my nervous system recalibrated to safety.

What we call PTSD might, in many cases, be an incomplete reintegration. A nervous system stuck mid-transition because it never got the chance to complete the cycle. Because the person never went back. Never proved to their body that they could handle both worlds. Never learned that the symptoms were temporary, not terminal.

I'm not saying trauma isn't real. I'm not dismissing what people carry. But I am saying this: reintegration is a skill. And like any skill, it gets easier with practice.

The first few times I came home, I felt lost. Broken, even. But by the twentieth, thirtieth deployment, I knew exactly what was happening. I could name the stages. Predict the timeline. Sit with the discomfort without panicking that it meant something was permanently wrong with me.

That knowledge changed everything.

During those years, the organization was growing. What started as a loose collective of volunteers filling gaps wherever we could now had structure. We filed the 501(c)(3), hired legal counsel, established internal oversight. It didn't make us immune to failure, but it gave us a framework.

And we needed it. Most nonprofits collapse under logistics, debt, infighting, or pure exhaustion. Starting a nonprofit is like being a gazelle in a den of lions. Funding dries up without warning. Volunteers burn out. Partnerships fall apart. One misstep and the whole thing dissolves.

But somehow, we were doing it. Slowly, unevenly, often one decision away from collapse, but doing it.

Our record was clean. Each deployment had landed without a major incident, and by conservative counts, the number of lives pulled back from the edge had climbed past several thousand. We hadn't chased attention, but it found us anyway—brief mentions at first, then headlines. Our name attached to the work others hesitated to touch. The places that were too unstable, too dangerous, too complicated.

What followed wasn't growth so much as momentum. Donors stayed. Not one-off checks, but people who returned, quietly, month after month. Private companies began calling—offering gear, pallets of supplies, sometimes aircraft or vehicles. No branding requirements, no strings attached. Just a question: Where do you need it?

And then there were the volunteers. They didn't come for money. They came because the work was honest. In a world full of abstraction, this was something solid. You could touch it. You could fail at it. You could save someone and know, without doubt, that it mattered.

That sense of reality was the glue. It held the whole thing together. The work wasn't pretty or stable, and it offered no guarantees, but it was real. And against all odds, it was working.

We weren't amateurs anymore—improvising our way through the unknown with borrowed gear and good intentions. We had infrastructure now. Systems. Delegation. Accountability. We were still lean, still allergic to bureaucracy, but we'd become something else: a dependable team that could land anywhere and start stabilizing chaos within hours.

Outside, the organization was finding its footing. Inside, I was still learning how to stand in two worlds without losing balance.

I'd been in a relationship during this period, and for a while we managed to keep it intact. She was patient, perceptive, sharper than most. But there are complications that patience alone can't fix.

I came home from Haiti on a Thursday afternoon. The flight had been delayed twice. I'd been awake for thirty-six hours.

She was waiting when I opened the door. The dog jumped up, tail going wild. She smiled, stepped forward to hug me.

"Hey. You're home."

"Yeah."

Her arms wrapped around me, but I felt stiff. Locked up. I hugged back, but it was mechanical. She pulled away, studying my face.

"You okay?"

"Just tired."

She nodded. "Dinner's ready. I made pasta."

I dropped my bag in the corner and followed her to the kitchen. The table was set. Candles lit. She'd made an effort.

I sat down. She poured wine, handed me a glass.

"How was it?"

"Fine."

"Just fine?"

I took a bite of salad. "Yeah. We helped some people. Did what we could."

She waited for more. I didn't offer it.

"I haven't seen you in three weeks. Can you give me more than 'fine'?"

I looked up. Her face was patient but tired. How many times had we done this? How many times had she asked for more and I'd given her less?

"There was a village. Cut off by a river. We got supplies in. Treated a few hundred people. It was good."

"That's amazing."

I nodded, eyes back on my plate.

The silence stretched. She sipped her wine. I ate mechanically.

"Are you staying this time?" she asked quietly.

"What do you mean?"

"I mean really staying. Not just physically here while your mind is already planning the next deployment."

I set down my fork. "I'm here."

"Are you?"

I didn't answer. Because she was right. Part of me was still in the last operation. Still running through supply manifests, checking radio batteries, mapping routes. Even sitting at this table, in this safe home, I was somewhere else.

She stood up, cleared her plate even though she'd barely eaten.

"I'm going to bed. I'm glad you're home safe."

She kissed the top of my head and left the room.

I sat there alone, staring at the candles she'd lit. The dog settled at my feet.

An hour later, I was in the corner, unpacking my bag, rotating batteries, checking gear for the next deployment.

The pattern repeated. Every homecoming looked the same. I'd try. She'd try. But the wall kept building.

Three weeks after I got back from South Sudan, she asked if we could talk.

We sat on the couch. The dog between us. She'd been quiet all evening.

"I can't do this anymore," she said.

I'd known it was coming. Maybe for months. But hearing it still hit.

"I know."

She looked at me, eyes red. "I love you. But you're never really here. And I don't think you know how to be."

"I'm trying."

"I know you are. But it's not enough. You leave every time your phone rings. And even when you stay, you're already gone."

I didn't argue. She was right.

"The work matters," I said. "People need—"

"I know it matters, I'm not asking you to stop. I'm just saying I can't be the person waiting anymore."

The silence stretched.

"I'm sorry," I said.

"So am I."

She stood up. Walked to the bedroom. Started packing a bag.

I sat there, knowing I should stop her, knowing I wouldn't.

An hour later, she was gone.

And then the phone rang.

Not a militia uprising. Not another hurricane. This time, it was a 7.5-magnitude earthquake in Indonesia, followed by a tsunami that swept entire neighborhoods into the sea. Communications down. Hospitals overwhelmed. Thousands unaccounted for.

The logistics officer on the other end didn't waste time.

"Can you deploy? We need a rescue team fast."

I looked around the room. The half-unpacked bag in the corner. The quiet apartment. Empty now.

I should have said no. I should have stayed. Tried to fix what I was breaking.

But thousands of people were unaccounted for. And I knew how to find them.

The choice wasn't really a choice. Not for me. Not anymore.

"Yes. Send me the details."

I wasn't leaving because I didn't know how to stay. I was leaving because—for better or worse—this was the place I belonged. And for now, that had to be enough. At least that's what I thought.

19

The Liquefaction

THE DESCENT INTO PALU offered no warning. From the air, the city looked like it had been scraped off the earth. Entire neighborhoods flattened, streets fractured and torn open, boats heaved inland like driftwood. The coastline had been redrawn, leaving a city buried under its own ruins.

After the tsunami alert buoys failed, the government ended warnings. People returned to their routines—work, school, daily life—unaware of what was coming. When the water struck, it spared no one near the coast. Boats, homes, families—swept away in seconds. Complete annihilation. Total erasure.

We touched down on a tarmac already packed with survivors and officials. The smell hit first: brine mixed with rot, sewage, and mud. People moved in waves, carrying what remained—babies, suitcases, photographs—pressing their hands, their stories, into us as if we could undo what had already happened.

Becca had arranged everything ahead of time—transport, local contacts, an immediate path into the city. Over the years I'd grown to rely on her with the same trust I put in my own hands. Waiting for us was our fixer, a woman Becca had coordinated with before we landed. She and her assistant guided us from the tarmac, navigating through the chaos and moving us straight into action.

Only three others accompanied me on this operation—each skilled, each aware that in a disaster zone, speed and precision could mean the difference between life and death. Our fixer led the way. English flawless, local knowledge unmatched. She guided us past fractured streets, leaning buildings, and debris fields, pointing out unstable structures, marking routes that could support our trucks, and identifying pockets where survivors had taken refuge. Every step was a calculation. Every glance at a ruined building or unstable wall demanded attention.

The city wasn't just destroyed—it was alive with motion. Local emergency teams were everywhere, sometimes chaotic, sometimes organized. People ran, carried, coordinated, shouted. We had to thread through this network, keeping track of not just our team but our objectives, supplies, and the vulnerable people we needed to reach.

Even in the disaster, doors opened to us. Officials—local and international—recognized skill and sought advice. At one site, a municipal officer flagged us down mid-ruins, explaining a neighborhood cut off from aid. Within minutes, we were directing resource allocation, coordinating with small rescue teams, and moving supplies into areas where others hesitated to go. The city's devastation created both chaos and a strange clarity—every decision mattered, and we could see the impact immediately.

After ensuring supplies reached the cut-off neighborhoods and the teams were in position, our fixer guided us away from the immediate chaos. She'd already arranged a place for us to rest—a mosque that had survived the worst, partially intact. Its walls bore deep scars, the dome had caved in at several points, and marble lay cracked beneath scattered debris, but it offered enough shelter to lay our heads. For the first time that day, we could stop moving, if only briefly.

As the sun lowered, shadows stretching across the fractured streets, we paused to regroup at a partially standing hospital. The scene was surreal: staff tending to survivors amid rubble, supplies stacked in corridors open to the sky. One of the volunteers looked at me, face drawn but alert. "Everywhere we go, it's the same story. Different city, same fight."

I nodded. There was a thread running through all of it—the human capacity to endure, to respond, to organize in chaos.

By nightfall, we'd hit dozens of sites, distributed medical aid, coordinated supply drops. We were exhausted. Muscles trembling from the work, minds still wired from making too many decisions too fast. But despite the fatigue, the stench, the horror all around us, there was a rhythm to it. A clarity that only comes when you know exactly what needs to be done and you have the skills to do it.

***

We collapsed at the mosque our fixer had arranged. I found a hard cot in the corner, laid down, and didn't move until morning.

The next day, I woke early despite the jet lag. We'd pushed hard the day before—skipped meals, barely slept—but I'd learned you can't operate on fumes. I made myself eat. Hydrate. Check gear. Small disciplines that keep you functional when things go sideways.

Our fixer came in while I was repacking my medical kit.

"They need help finding the bodies." Her breath was sharp, urgent.

I looked up. "What bodies?"

She swallowed. "A mosque collapsed inside the liquefaction zone. Hundreds of children were buried."

I set the kit down. "Liquefaction zone?"

She nodded. "It's still active. Aftershocks every few hours. The ground isn't stable."

Corey was already listening. I could see him running the same calculations I was.

"How unstable?" I asked.

"They've lost two excavators already. Sunk into the mud. The operators barely got out."

I pulled out my notebook—something I'd started doing after Oklahoma. Write it down. Map the variables. Don't just react.

"How many children?"

"Hundreds. They don't know."

I wrote that down. Underlined it. Then I started listing what we'd need to know:

Exact location

Last aftershock timing

Soil composition

Depth of collapse

Available equipment

Local expertise on liquefaction

Corey leaned over, reading my list. "We're not excavator operators."

"No. But we can assess. See if there's a way in that doesn't require heavy machinery."

"And if there isn't?"

I thought about the risk. Thought about what happens when the ground turns to liquid beneath your feet. Thought about aftershocks hitting while you're waist-deep in mud with no way out.

Then I thought about those kids buried under thirty feet of earth.

"We go look first. We assess. If it's a death trap, we walk away and find another way to help. But we don't say no before we see it."

Corey nodded. That was the protocol we'd developed: assess before committing. Never promise what you can't deliver. Never take risks that turn you into another casualty.

"We'll go," I told the fixer. "But we're not making promises until we see the site."

This was my first time confronting a liquefaction zone. It occurs when violent shaking forces water-saturated soil to lose its strength and behave like a liquid. The earthquake had struck first, the ground convulsing hard enough to rupture deep pockets of groundwater. When those pockets burst upward, the soil lost its structure. Neighborhoods turned into something closer to quicksand.

Only after the quake did the tsunami arrive, pushing seawater far inland and worsening the saturation. What had already been unstable ground became a churning mess of mud, water, and debris.

The effect was catastrophic. Streets and neighborhoods didn't simply fracture—they dropped, sometimes twenty feet in seconds. Houses folded in on themselves. Buildings twisted as if softened by heat. Cars, trees, even small boats were lifted and rolled in slow arcs. The destruction followed no pattern. It radiated in erratic sweeps, displacing entire communities up to a mile from where they had stood.

And it was still happening.

Aftershocks hit every few hours. Each one strong enough to reactivate the liquefaction. The ground would shudder, lose cohesion, and anything standing on it—excavators, people, buildings—would sink. Two pieces of heavy equipment had already been swallowed whole.

We gathered the team before heading out. Corey, our fixer, the volunteers who'd flown in with us. I laid it out straight.

"The zone is active. If a tremor hits while we're in there, the ground won't hold us. We'll have maybe thirty seconds to get to solid ground. Maybe less. Two excavators have already been swallowed. The operators barely made it out."

I let that sink in.

"We're going to assess first. See what's possible. But I need everyone to understand: this isn't a standard operation. The risk is real. If you want to sit this one out, no judgment. No hard feelings. You stay here, help coordinate from the edge. That's valuable work too."

No one moved.

Corey spoke first. "I'm in."

The volunteers nodded. One by one, they confirmed.

"All right," I said. "Same rules apply. We assess. If it's too dangerous, we pull back and find another way to help. We don't take risks that turn us into casualties. Clear?"

Everyone nodded.

"Let's move."

We rose and pulled together what we needed. The driver was already idling near the treeline, and we climbed into the truck. He pushed the pace, the tires sliding through ruts of wet clay. Along the way the scale of the damage pressed in from every direction. Families had staked out pockets of high ground, stretching linens between branches to form temporary shelters. Men hauled debris out of the roads. Children stood in loose clusters near pallets of water that had just been dropped off.

What struck me was the absence of anyone from the usual global outfits. A place hit this hard would normally be crowded with them, but everything here was being handled by the local municipalities and Indonesia's BNPB. I leaned toward our fixer.

"Why so few outside teams?"

She watched the road a moment before answering. "I was surprised you made it in at all."

"What's keeping them out?"

"The prison collapsed. It held several high-risk ISIS militants. Most escaped. Until they're accounted for, the government doesn't want foreign teams becoming targets. One incident would turn this into a diplomatic mess."

Corey and I let that settle. The entire island was only 152 square miles. Hard to blame them for tightening access.

HARP carried real credibility. Our reputation preceded us, and it was almost certainly the reason we were cleared into Palu ahead of most others. There were only a handful of teams in the world doing this kind of work at that level—one or two at most—and even fewer who specialized in moving fast, light, and directly into unstable ground. For better or worse, we were part of the original lineage of modern humanitarian rescue, built before the playbooks existed.

That kind of standing opens doors quietly. No announcements. Just a nod, a clearance, a runway that others didn't yet have. But early access isn't comfort—it's exposure. There's no aid corridor to blend into, no safety in numbers, no one else setting the tempo. If something goes wrong, it's on you. If something works, it becomes the model others follow.

Being first meant operating without insulation. Fewer buffers. Fewer redundancies. Every decision carried consequence beyond the immediate moment, because it shaped how the entire response would unfold.

Reputation buys entry. What you do once you're inside determines whether the door stays open.

After about twenty minutes weaving through side streets and mud-laden paths, we reached a clearing where the paved road ended. Not because the road stopped—but because it no longer existed. This was the boundary between the ordinary world and the liquefaction zone.

We climbed from the vehicle, securing our packs. The driver and our fixer stayed behind. Even from the edge, the ground shuddered underfoot—reminders of the aftershocks still moving through the earth.

I took a step forward. The mud shifted beneath my boot, unstable, unpredictable. I could feel it—the ground wasn't solid. It moved like something alive, responding to pressure, to weight.

Corey stepped beside me. "You feel that?"

"Yeah."

"If a tremor hits—"

"I know."

We both knew. If the ground started liquefying while we were out there, we'd have seconds to react. Maybe not even that. The mud would turn from semi-solid to liquid in an instant. You'd sink fast. And if you were deep in a pit when it happened, pulling bodies out, you wouldn't make it to the edge in time.

But those kids were out there. Buried. Waiting.

"Let's move," I said.

Everything beyond this line was an unknown variable.

Palm trees, normally twenty to thirty feet high, barely jutted above the mud as if trimmed to their crowns. Homes were splintered and twisted. Vehicles half-buried, half-floating—nothing aligned, nothing familiar. The mud had swallowed, churned, lifted, and tossed everything.

"Look, in the distance." The fixer pointed. "See the tall building—the one with the gold on top?"

Corey and I followed her gaze. There it was: the structure leaning heavily to one side.

"Yeah, I see it."

"That's the school—the mosque. Get there. They'll know who you are."

And just like that, Corey, the volunteers, and I began our slow trek toward the building, each step deliberate, every glance scanning for danger or instability, the mud groaning beneath us.

What should have taken twenty minutes stretched into nearly an hour. There was no path—only a scramble over the remnants of lives. Homes stacked on cars, cars buried under homes, everything half-submerged, half-twisted. Nothing was where it should be. The mud had reshuffled an entire neighborhood like a deck of cards.

I'd seen catastrophic damage before. Earthquakes. Hurricanes. War zones. This was different. This wasn't destruction—it was erasure and reassembly. The landscape had been disassembled and put back together wrong.

When we reached the site, the scene struck us silent. Roughly a dozen men worked alongside a single excavator, digging through mounds of mud. The holes plunged some thirty feet deep. At the bottom, men hauled what remained of the buried upward, carefully, as if the slightest misstep could erase what little dignity remained.

I stopped at the edge, watching. Assessing.

The excavator was operating at the perimeter of the zone, not in the deepest part. Smart. The men working the pit had a system—rotating in and out, never more than two at the bottom at once. Exit paths were clear. They'd marked stable ground with stakes and rope.

I looked at Corey. "They've figured out how to work it safely. Small teams. Quick rotations. Stay near the edges."

He nodded, reading the same things I was. "Manageable."

"The risk is still there. An aftershock hits, we're all in trouble."

"But they're already doing it," Corey said. "They need more hands. We can help without making it more dangerous."

I watched the men work for another minute. The ground was treacherous, but it wasn't a suicide mission. They'd found a way.

"All right. We're in. But we follow their system. We don't improvise. We rotate out regularly. First sign of a tremor, everyone gets to high ground immediately."

Corey nodded.

One man broke from the group and approached.

"You're the rescue group?"

I nodded. "We're here to help."

The others remained frozen, eyes fixed on the task before them.

"Please, follow me. There are so many." He moved swiftly toward one of the large pits already dug, and we followed, descending into the mud-filled grave.

The remainder of the day blurred into relentless motion. We pulled bodies from the mud—mostly children, over sixty in total. Each one had been swallowed by the earth, buried beneath twisted metal and churned soil. Most were no older than thirteen.

They were cold to the touch, the mud preserving them in stillness. Hands and faces, once warm and alive, now weighted by earth.

Each lift of a small body was a battle against the sucking mud, each step back up the slick banks a test of balance and strength. My boots sank, mud pulling at ankles and calves, fingers raw from grit and repeated strain. The heat of the day pressed down on us, sweat mixing with the grime of the work, but it did nothing to dull the chill of what we carried.

There was no time to process each life lost. Yet each one stayed—the curve of a cheek, a hand still curled, the weight of a small body that once had hopes and laughter. Our muscles ached, lungs burned, and still we continued.

By evening, our hands were cracked, stained, and trembling, but we had not stopped. The line of the dead stretched behind us. And yet, amid the horror, there was a strange quiet in moving deliberately, giving names and faces back to those who had been claimed by silence.

We hiked out at dusk. The ground shivered beneath our boots, subtle tremors rising and falling. Mud clung to our soles, slick and untrustworthy. No one spoke. Every footfall echoed the day's events. Faces were streaked with grime, eyes vacant yet sharp.

The air smelled of wet earth, decay, and dust. Somewhere in the distance, a branch snapped, startling a bird, and the sudden chirp sounded too bright against the silence.

We didn't talk on the drive back. There was nothing to say.

20

Cut Off

I N THE DAYS THAT followed, our work pushed outward from the city into the surrounding hills. Damage radiated beyond the island, cutting off villages, folding roads into the landscape. Reaching them meant moving through terrain that no longer behaved like terrain. Slopes sagged. Pavement ended without warning. The ground carried a low, unsettled tension, as if it were still deciding where to fail.

One assignment took us toward a village on the east side of the island. A landslide had buried one of the main roads, sealing off everything beyond it. Traffic had backed up on both sides. People stood outside their cars in loose clusters, watching the hillside from a distance, waiting for someone to decide what would happen next.

The slide rose hundreds of feet above the road. The mud was still dark and wet, heavy with water, its surface creased and uneven. Two bulldozers were working high on the slope, small against the scale of the hill, their tracks cut into the slide itself.

From where we stood, the machines looked almost suspended, perched beneath the remaining mass of earth. Above them, the hillside bulged outward, fractured and tense, as if held in place by habit rather than physics.

I stepped forward until my boots sank several inches into the mud. The ground shifted constantly, not enough to knock me off balance, but enough to register. Aftershocks moved through the slope like pulses. Nothing had settled.

I turned to the nearest official. "They need to come down. Now. It's not safe."

He looked at me, then at the bulldozers.

"The road needs to be cleared," he said.

"The road can wait. That slope is going to fail."

I pointed to the upper face of the slide, to the weight still hanging above the machines. "See that bulge? That's the fracture line. When it goes, it'll take everything below it. Those men won't have time to react."

He hesitated. Looked up at the bulldozers again. The engines continued to work, metal arms rising and falling in slow, deliberate arcs.

"How long do they have?" he asked.

"I don't know. Could be an hour. Could be the next aftershock."

He nodded slowly. But he didn't call them down.

I repeated myself, louder this time, pointing out where the failure would start, how it would travel, how little warning there would be. The men in the excavators were too far away to hear. The engines kept working.

No one ordered them to stop.

Time stretched. People along the road fell silent. Some shaded their eyes, watching. Others turned away, unwilling to witness what they already sensed. The hillside loomed above it all, unreadable, indifferent.

Then the ground tightened.

An aftershock passed through, sharper than the others. From the road, the slope rippled—a subtle wave running through the mud.

"Get back!" I shouted.

But the men in the bulldozers couldn't hear me. The engines kept working, metal arms rising and falling.

The hillside released.

The slide surged downward as a single mass, swallowing both bulldozers mid-motion. No warning. No time to react. One second they were there, the next they were gone. The engines disappeared, cut off by the weight of earth. When it stopped, the slope had smoothed itself. The road was gone. The machines were gone.

The hillside looked quiet. Almost finished.

No one moved. No one spoke.

Then a woman screamed.

She broke from the crowd, running toward the slope, stumbling through the mud. Her voice tore through the silence—raw, desperate, the kind of sound that only comes when the world breaks in front of you.

Someone caught her before she reached the slide. She fought against them, arms reaching toward the smooth mud where the bulldozers had been, as if she could pull them back by force of will alone.

"My husband! My husband is in there! Please!"

She turned toward us, toward me, her face streaked with tears and mud. "Please! You have to get him out! Please!"

I stood there, frozen. Every instinct told me to move, to do something, to try. But my feet wouldn't move.

One of the local officials approached, face tight. He looked at me, then at the woman still screaming, still fighting to get to the slope.

"Can you reach them?" he asked quietly.

I looked at the slope. At the fresh mud still settling. At the aftershocks still moving through the ground.

"How deep?" Corey asked beside me.

"Twenty feet. Maybe more."

The woman heard us. She pulled free from whoever was holding her and came toward me, hands reaching, gripping my arm.

"Please. He's in there. He could still be alive. Please."

I looked at her. At the desperation in her eyes. At the hope she was clinging to because she had nothing else left.

I did the math. Two men. Enclosed cabs. If the mud hadn't crushed them immediately, if there were air pockets, if they'd survived the impact—maybe they had minutes. Maybe.

But reaching them would mean digging through unstable mud in an active slide zone with aftershocks hitting every few hours. We'd need heavy equipment. The same equipment that just got swallowed.

If we went in, we'd die too. And they'd still be gone.

"I'm sorry," I said.

Her face changed. Hope collapsed into something worse—understanding. She knew what I was saying.

"No," she said. "No. Please. You have to try. Please."

"I can't. We can't reach them. The ground won't hold."

"He's alive! I know he's alive!" Her voice broke. "Please don't leave him there. Please."

I looked at Corey. He was staring at the mud, jaw tight.

I turned back to her. "If we go in, we die too. And he still dies. I can't—I can't ask my team to do that."

She collapsed. Someone caught her before she hit the ground. Her sobs were the only sound—ragged, broken, the kind that don't stop because there's nothing left to hold them back.

The official looked at me. Waiting for me to change my mind. Waiting for me to say something different.

I didn't.

"We can't reach them," I said again. Firm enough to end the conversation.

He nodded slowly. He'd already known. He just needed someone else to say it.

I looked at the smooth mud one more time. Somewhere underneath, thirty feet down, two men were either already dead or dying. And I was choosing not to try.

The woman was still crying. Still reaching toward the slope like she could bring him back.

I turned away. Because if I kept looking at her, I'd doubt the decision. And the decision was right.

It had to be.

We stood there for another minute. Then we walked back to the trucks.

Behind us, the woman's sobs faded into the distance. But not far enough.

They never do.

***

Within the hour, we found a way around the blockage, navigating narrow dirt paths, fractured terrain, and mud-slicked slopes. Every turn carried uncertainty—one misstep, one hidden drop, could undo the progress we'd made.

By late morning, we reached the first of two villages cut off by the landslide. The road narrowed and buckled as our two trucks pushed forward, tires sliding over broken asphalt and mud still wet from rain and aftershocks. Windows were down. Engines stayed low. We listened as much as we drove, alert to any sound from the slope above that didn't belong.

When we rolled into the village, people emerged cautiously from what remained of their homes. No one ran. They watched the trucks first, measuring intent. Then they stepped forward—families framed by fractured walls and sagging roofs, hands gripping what little they could carry.

We made it clear quickly who we could take. Only the injured. Only the sick. The limits were hard, and everyone understood them without argument. Mothers guided children forward who were burning with fever. Men supported elders who could no longer stand on their own. Wounds were uncovered without drama, infections revealed quietly, as if dignity still mattered even here.

We positioned the trucks where the ground felt most stable. The injured were loaded first, lifted carefully into the beds, eased onto benches padded with whatever we had. The sick followed, movements slow, controlled, deliberate. There was no panic, only urgency restrained by care. Those staying behind stood back, watching, already preparing for what came next.

The second village lay farther along the compromised road. Getting there meant committing to a stretch of terrain where turning back was not an option. We drove it steadily, neither rushing nor hesitating, aware that momentum itself was a form of safety. The village was smaller, more exposed. Days without food or clean water had left their mark. Dehydration showed in the eyes. Illness moved unchecked through crowded shelters.

Again, we made the same assessment. Again, the same quiet acceptance. Those who needed immediate care were brought forward. In total, 22 people—sick, injured, failing—were loaded into the trucks. The rest stood aside, offering help where they could, steadying arms, lifting legs, pressing hands together in gestures that carried more than words.

We were close enough to the coastline to make a cleaner choice. Rather than pressing farther inland with injured people in the trucks, rather than gambling their lives against unstable roads and uncertain ground, we turned toward the sea. Just offshore, a large hospital ship lay anchored, its white hull steady against the shifting land, staffed and ready. It gave us a fixed point in a landscape that refused to hold still.

We drove the trucks out along the last stretch of passable road, keeping speed constant, avoiding sudden braking, every movement deliberate. The injured rode quietly, wrapped tight, conserving what little strength they had left.

The trucks pulled in beside a small transfer clinic set up near the coast. Doctors and volunteers were already in motion as we arrived, moving with the calm precision that only comes from repetition and trust. The injured were triaged immediately. Fevers were brought down. Dehydration addressed. Wounds cleaned and reassessed. Food was passed hand to hand. Blankets were wrapped tight around shaking shoulders.

From there, patients were moved in stages to the ship offshore, ferried toward proper operating rooms, stable power, and supplies that would not run out overnight. Bodies that had been failing began, slowly, to stabilize—not because the disaster had eased, but because we had stopped forcing our way through it.

It was a reminder that rescue is not always about pushing ahead. Sometimes it's about knowing when to stop, where to hand off, and how to keep people alive without demanding more from them than they can give.

For the first time in days, there was rest. Strength returned in increments. Quiet smiles appeared—not relief, exactly, but recognition. They had been seen. They had been reached.

***

That night, we gathered around a fire as local volunteers joined us. Some brought food. Some brought stories. Some brought grief they had nowhere else to put. The flames moved across exhausted faces, shadows rising and falling with each shift of the fire. Care passed quietly—water refilled, blankets shared, silence respected.

No one mentioned the bulldozers directly. But everyone was thinking about it.

One of the volunteers finally spoke. "Could we have reached them?"

I shook my head. "No. Not without losing people."

"But if there was a chance—"

"There wasn't." I said it firm enough to end the conversation.

But the question stayed. It always does.

Being in a place where saving life should be the central measure of action—and then making the choice to let life slip away—is a burden that never goes away.

Those men died because someone decided moving traffic was more important than waiting for the slope to stabilize. And I chose not to risk more lives trying to undo that mistake.

The decision was right. I know that.

But I still see the smooth mud where they disappeared. I still hear the woman's voice, breaking as she begged me to try. I still feel her hands gripping my arm.

And I carry that.

Some of the volunteers were new. They listened closely, absorbing what this kind of work demands and what it takes in return. Few stay long. That reckoning could wait.

For that night, there was only the fire, shared exhaustion, and the steady presence of people committed to one another in a place where commitment still mattered.

***

Our time in Palu ended a few days later. The aftershocks had softened into long, distant tremors, more reminder than threat. The urgency that had defined every hour began to ease, replaced by a steadier rhythm as the final rescues drew toward completion. Fewer sirens cut the air. Fewer bodies were carried. The city, though still broken, had begun the slow work of holding itself together.

The people we had reached were accounted for. The injured were treated. The sick stabilized. No one under our care had been lost. In a place where loss had arrived in waves, that fact carried quiet significance. It wasn't victory—nothing here resembled that—but it was resolution.

Local teams continued the work now reinforced by broader international support. Systems replaced improvisation. Supply lines stabilized. What had begun in chaos was finding structure. We stepped back not because the need had vanished, but because the response no longer required us to be in the way.

Before we left, representatives from the Indonesian government acknowledged our role in the medical and rescue operations. There were no speeches—just handshakes, brief words, and an understanding shared without embellishment. We had come when access was limited, moved quickly, and left without demanding recognition. That, too, was part of the work.

We left knowing that what we had done would not define the city's recovery. It would simply become part of its early hours—those fragile days when outcomes were uncertain and decisions carried consequences that could not be reversed. In that narrow window, we had acted with care, restraint, and purpose.

Sometimes that is all you are given.

21

Nine Months

THE PHONE RANG ON a Tuesday afternoon, three months after Indonesia.

I almost didn't answer. Unknown number. Probably another logistics coordinator, another interview request I'd decline, another pitch for something I didn't need.

But I picked up anyway.

"This is Grace Kane. I'm a journalist working on a story about humanitarian organizations operating in high-risk zones. I was hoping to ask you a few questions about HARP and this type of work... if you have the time."

I'd done interviews before. They usually lasted ten minutes. Surface-level questions about "what it's like" and "why you do it" that never got past the script. I expected the same.

"Sure. What do you want to know?"

"I read about your work in Indonesia. That was you and your team, right?"

"Yeah."

"Can I ask—how do you make the call? When it's too dangerous to go in?"

I stopped. Most journalists asked about the rescues. The successes. Not the failures. Not the calls you don't make.

"What do you mean?"

"I read that two men were buried when the bulldozers went under. And your team didn't attempt recovery. I'm not criticizing—I'm asking how you make that decision. How do you choose not to try?"

The question landed differently than I expected. Not accusatory. Just curious. Genuine.

"You do the math," I said. "Chance of success versus chance of losing everyone. If the math doesn't work, you don't go in."

"But how do you calculate that? In the moment?"

I thought about how to explain it. "You start with what you know. Soil stability. Weather. Equipment available. Team experience. You list the variables you can measure."

"And the ones you can't?"

"That's where it gets harder. Unknown variables usually dominate the space. The ground might hold. It might not. The aftershock might come in an hour. Might come in thirty seconds. You're making decisions based on incomplete information that's constantly changing."

"So how do you decide?"

"You learn to trust patterns. You've seen enough situations that you start recognizing when something's manageable versus when it's a death trap. You weigh the odds based on experience. Sometimes the variables change so fast you don't have time to recalculate—you just have to trust your instincts."

Silence on the other end. Then: "And when your instincts say no?"

"Then you don't go. Even when people are dying. Even when you know you could maybe reach them. Because if you lose your team trying, you've just created more bodies to recover and no one left to help the next person."

"But how do you live with that? Knowing you made the right call but it still cost lives?"

No one had ever asked me that. Not directly.

I paused for a long moment.

"You just do," I said. "Because the alternative is worse."

Silence on the other end. Not awkward. Thoughtful.

"That sounds lonely."

It was. But I didn't say that.

"It comes with the work," I said.

"Does it have to?"

The question hung there. I didn't have a good answer.

"Maybe not. But when you're standing there, making the call, you're the only one who has to live with it. The team trusts you to make the right decision. The people you can't save don't get a vote. And the people back home who weren't there—they don't understand the variables. So yeah. It's lonely."

"Do you ever second-guess yourself? After?"

"Always. Every time I say no, I wonder if I was wrong. If there was something I missed. Some way we could have made it work."

"And when you're right? When you make the call and it saves your team?"

"Then I'm grateful. But I'm also carrying the weight of who-ever we left behind."

Another pause. Longer this time.

"How do you keep doing it?"

"Because the alternative is doing nothing. And that's worse."

We talked for an hour. Then two. She asked about the things no one asks about—the reintegration, the isolation, the relationships that fail because you can't explain why you keep leaving. She didn't romanticize it. She didn't flinch from it. She just listened.

When we finally hung up, I sat there for a long time, staring at my phone.

***

She called back the next day.

"I have more questions," she said. "If you have time."

I had time.

Over the next six months, we spoke almost daily. Sometimes once. Sometimes three or four times. She was working on the story, yes, but the conversations drifted beyond that quickly.

She asked about the operations I didn't talk about. The ones that went wrong. The ones where I second-guessed every choice for weeks afterward. She asked about the volunteers who burned out, the donors who disappeared, the moments when I thought about walking away.

And she told me about her work. The stories she'd covered. The people she'd met. The cost of witnessing suffering without being able to fix it.

"It's different for you," I said one night. "You report it. I'm supposed to stop it."

"Are you, though?"

"What do you mean?"

"You can't stop all of it. No one can. So why do you hold yourself to that standard?"

I didn't have an answer. Or maybe I did, and I just didn't want to say it out loud.

"Because if I don't," I said finally, "then what's the point?"

"The point is that you show up anyway. Even when you know you can't save everyone. That's the point."

It was the first time anyone had said that to me. The first time it didn't feel like failure.

***

A few weeks into our conversations, I left for a small operation. Nothing major—a flood in Central America, mostly logistics and supply distribution. I was gone for ten days.

She called every night.

Not to check in. Not to reassure herself I was alive. Just to talk. About the work, about the day, about nothing in particular. Her voice became the thing I looked forward to after long days in the mud.

When I got back, she was the first person I called.

"How was it?" she asked.

"Wet. Exhausting. Successful."

"Good."

A pause.

"I missed talking to you," I said.

"I missed it too."

Another pause. Longer this time.

"When can I see you?" she asked.

"Whenever you want."

***

We met in person two weeks later. She flew out to meet me halfway—a small city neither of us had been to before. Neutral ground.

I was nervous. I hadn't been nervous in years.

She walked into the coffee shop, and I recognized her immediately. Not from a photo—we hadn't exchanged any. But from her voice. From the way she carried herself. Steady. Present. Unhurried.

"Hi," she said.

"Hi."

We sat down. Ordered coffee. And then we just talked. The same way we had on the phone, but better. Because I could see her now. The way she listened. The way she smiled when I said something she hadn't expected. The way she leaned in when the conversation turned serious.

Hours passed. The coffee shop closed. We moved to a park, walked until the streetlights came on, then kept walking.

"Can I ask you something?" she said.

"Yeah."

"Why do you do this? The real reason. Not the press release version."

I thought about it. Really thought about it.

The real reason was something I'd never said out loud. Something I wasn't ready to share. Not yet. Maybe not ever.

"Because I can," I said. "Because I have the skills, the experience, the team. And if I don't use them, people die who didn't have to."

"But at what cost to you?"

"I don't know. I haven't figured that out yet."

She stopped walking. Turned to face me.

"Maybe it's time you did."

Over the next three months, we saw each other as often as we could. She'd fly out. I'd fly to her. We'd meet in random cities and spend weekends walking, talking, eating terrible food, laughing at things that weren't that funny.

She understood the rhythm of my life in a way no one else had. When I left for operations, she didn't panic. She didn't demand reassurance. She just said, "Be safe. Call when you can."

And when I came back, she didn't ask me to be someone I wasn't. She didn't try to fix me or save me or convince me to stop. She just made space for me to exist exactly as I was.

***

One night, sitting on her couch after a particularly brutal operation in Southeast Asia, I said something I hadn't planned to say.

"I love you."

She looked at me. Didn't smile. Didn't look surprised. Just nodded.

"I know. I love you too."

"You know?"

"I've known for a while."

"Why didn't you say anything?"

"I was waiting for you to figure it out."

I laughed. For the first time in weeks, I laughed.

***

By the ninth month, we'd stopped pretending distance was sustainable.

"Move in with me," she said one morning over coffee.

I looked at her. "You sure?"

"I'm sure. Are you?"

I thought about it. Thought about what it would mean. The compromise. The vulnerability. The risk of letting someone that close.

"Yeah," I said. "I'm sure."

We moved in together two weeks later. No fanfare. No big declarations. Just two people folding their lives together because it made more sense than keeping them apart.

The house was small. Too small, really. But it didn't matter. For the first time in years, I had a place that felt like more than shelter. I had a home.

Mornings became rituals. Coffee brewed while she showered. Breakfast made together in a kitchen barely big enough for one person, let alone two. Evenings stretched longer than they needed to, filled with cooking, talking, laughing at nothing in particular.

She learned my rhythms. When to ask questions and when to let silence do the work. When to push and when to give me space. When to remind me that I didn't have to carry everything alone.

And I learned hers. The way she needed quiet in the mornings. The way she processed stress by moving—walking, running, cleaning. The way she'd reach for my hand without thinking, like it was the most natural thing in the world.

For the first time in my life, I understood what people meant when they said "home."

It wasn't a place. It was a person.

***

Three weeks after we moved in together, the phone rang.

I was in the kitchen. She was on the couch, reading. The sound cut through the room like it always did—sharp, insistent, impossible to ignore.

I looked at the screen. Recognized the number.

She looked up. Our eyes met. She knew what it meant.

I answered.

"We need you. Can you deploy?"

I looked at her. She was watching me, face calm but eyes alert.

"When?" I asked.

"Seventy-two hours. Maybe less."

I closed my eyes. Took a breath.

"I'll call you back in ten minutes."

I hung up.

She set her book down. Waited.

I sat down beside her. Took her hand.

"I have to go."

"I know."

We sat there for a long time. Not speaking. Just holding on.

Finally, she broke the silence.

"Come back."

"I will."

"Promise me."

I looked at her. At the life we'd built in nine months. At the future I'd started to believe was possible.

"I promise. And when I get back... I'm going to start finding a way out."

She looked at me. "What do you mean?"

"I mean I can't keep doing this forever. I can't keep leaving. I can't ask you to build a life around absence and risk. So when I come back, I start transitioning. Writing. Teaching. Speaking. Finding a way to do this work without stepping into the fire every time."

Her face softened. Relief, maybe. Or hope.

"You mean that?"

"Yeah. I do."

She leaned into me. I wrapped my arms around her.

"Then go," she said quietly. "Do what you need to do. And come back to me."

The next morning, I packed my gear. Boots laced. Bag ready. She stood in the doorway, watching.

"Be safe," she said.

"I will."

"I love you."

"I love you too."

I kissed her. Held her longer than I needed to. Then I left.

But this time was different.

This time, I wasn't just leaving. I was coming back to something. To someone.

For the first time in my life, I had something worth coming home to.

And I wasn't going to let it go.

22

The Collision

W E SAT ON THE tarmac in Miami beneath a sun that wouldn't quit. Heat rose off the concrete in waves. Sweat pooled and evaporated just as fast. My team spread out beside me, backs against duffels and hard cases, conserving energy, speaking only when necessary. We were waiting.

This was the mission. The one I'd promised Grace I'd come back from and start transitioning out. Abaco. Hurricane Dorian had just torn through the Bahamas, and they needed a team fast.

After half an hour, the helicopter appeared through the haze. A retired military bird, scarred and loud, dropping low over the runway before settling. Rotors thrashed the air. The team moved immediately. Gear first. Then bodies. No wasted motion. Shoulder to shoulder, knees pressed into packs, head-sets crackling. I gave the pilot a thumbs-up. He nodded. We lifted.

The flight took just over an hour. From above, scattered coral reefs and white sandbars cut the water into blues and greens. The Gulf Stream stretched beneath us, leading to the boomerang-shaped archipelago of Great Abaco. From the air, the ocean looked calm, a wide expanse of blue. Then the island appeared.

Abaco looked torn apart. A thin strip of land caught between beauty and destruction. The water remained turquoise, still inviting, but the shoreline had been ripped to pieces. Wreckage floated in the shallows—roofs, boats, fragments of lives where homes had stood just days before.

As we flew lower, the scale sharpened. Neighborhoods erased. Streets dissolved into channels of brown water. Foundations stripped bare. The island didn't just look damaged. It looked gutted.

We had coordinates. Nothing more. Latitude and longitude scribbled hastily on a pad, which I handed to the pilot. He entered them into the control display. The helicopter banked wide, engines humming.

When we reached the target, he circled slowly, searching for anything that looked like solid ground. From this height, it was hard to tell what was land, what was water, what had been swallowed or carried away. Palm trees lay broken, their fronds scattered. Tin roofs had been ripped loose, twisting in the wind before settling in heaps.

Finally, the pilot's eyes narrowed. His hand hovered over the controls, then pointed. A small patch of land rose above the water. Barely a handful of acres, but enough. An island within an island.

He brought us down carefully.

The helicopter touched down near the hospital coordinates, throwing up a spray of dust, debris, and salt. The building stood half-submerged, its walls bulging with trapped water, ceilings sagging, windows shattered. The storm had gutted everything inside.

We stepped off and were immediately met by local volunteers—faces lined with exhaustion, hands already moving to help. They led us to the hospital, where others were already at work boarding up shattered windows, sweeping out seawater that had climbed three feet up the walls. We found a dry room and dropped our gear. This would be home.

The first days blurred. Half the team waded through the hospital's corridors, tearing away mold-streaked drywall, tossing out waterlogged equipment, flushing stagnant pools. The air reeked of mildew and rot. Another group tackled the generator—the diesel engine submerged in saltwater, bolts seized, wires corroded. We dismantled it piece by piece, improvising with scavenged parts. Power meant lights, refrigeration, medical devices. Power meant hope.

The third team fanned out beyond the hospital, moving through streets and makeshift shelters, searching for the dead and tending to the bedridden who had survived—barely. Triage became instinct: a hydration bag here, an antibiotic there, hands steady even as exhaustion pulled at us. Bodies were recovered with care, placed in the morgue freezer behind the hospital.

We set up a radio network so the teams could communicate across the island. Small transmitters placed on roof edges, propped atop rubble, tucked into corners with clear sightlines. As the network came online, radios crackled and lights blinked. For the first time since landing, we had eyes on one another.

***

Days bled into one another. The island swallowed time—long, sweating hours blurred by the sheer volume of need. Eventually, the people stopped seeing us as responders. We weren't guests anymore. We were relied upon.

And that reliance wasn't always medical. Sometimes it was emotional. Sometimes logistical. Sometimes it was just a desperate knock at an hour when the world still pretended it should be asleep.

It was early—too early. 5:30 a.m. by my watch. I'd just started drifting when the knock came. Loud. Urgent. Fist on wood, over and over.

I stumbled to the door, heart already climbing. One of the local nurses stood there—eyes wide, face pale. She didn't wait for me to speak.

"We need you. There's been a car accident—about a mile out. It's bad."

I was already pulling on my pants. "How many?"

"I don't know. Two cars. They went head on. One flipped."

That was all I needed.

I grabbed the medical jump bag and slammed the door behind me. Corey met me in the hall, already dressed.

"Let's move."

We grabbed one more teammate and piled into the truck. Tires spat gravel as we tore down the barely lit road. The sun hadn't broken the horizon yet, but the world had begun turning gray.

A flicker of headlights up ahead. Several vehicles clustered together. We slowed, the scene unfolding piece by piece.

Two vehicles—what was left of them. A flipped truck, twisted and torn. A car crushed, its front end folded like paper. The story was written—head-on, sudden, violent. Smoke curled upward, thick and lazy.

We jumped out and moved fast. No sirens. No bystanders with phones out. Just locals, silent and stunned. One man vomited into the grass. Another stood barefoot, holding his head in both hands.

I went to the flipped truck first. Glass crunched underfoot. The driver was pinned, blood smeared across the ceiling—what was now the floor. Breathing. Barely.

"Corey, airway." My voice was tight, sharp. He slid in beside the man, careful, precise.

"Hey, buddy." I leaned close, forcing my voice steady. His eyes barely opened, glassy and distant. "I'm gonna get you out, okay? Just hang on."

He nodded, slow, almost imperceptible. Too quiet. Shock was already taking over. Blood streaked across his temple from a jagged cut. His left femur was snapped clean.

Corey worked methodically, checking the airway. He pulled a pocket knife, slicing through the seatbelt that had pinned the man. Every movement mattered. Every second could tip the balance.

I kept talking, a low, constant hum of reassurance. "You're okay. You're okay. We've got you."

Once we had him stable enough to move, we lifted carefully and placed him into the back of a truck. Every step deliberate, every heartbeat a countdown.

I barked orders. "Get him to the hospital—fast. Before shock sets in!"

The truck tore off, tires biting into the road, kicking up dust.

The other car was worse. Driver and passenger slumped over the dash, unconscious. Two in the backseat—mid-twenties—also out cold. Or worse.

This one hit harder.

The metal looked like it had melted and re-formed around them.

The driver—impaled on the steering wheel, spine bent wrong. The passenger had gone face-first into the dash. I couldn't tell where he ended and the plastic began.

I crawled into the back. One man's neck told me everything I didn't want to know. I kicked out what remained of the back window and climbed inside.

I reached for wrists.

No pulse. No breath.

Gone.

I let out a breath I didn't know I'd been holding.

Corey was watching me from the side door.

"They're gone."

He nodded. He already knew.

We unstrapped them, one at a time, lifting them out carefully. Corey laid them beside each other. No words. None needed.

Back in the truck, I grabbed the reciprocating saw we'd tossed in the trunk days earlier. Just in case. This was the case.

I returned and started cutting through the passenger door—metal shrieking against blade. I felt every vibration in my arms, each one a reminder that we weren't supposed to be doing this. But there was no one else.

We got the passenger out. Laid him beside the others. Three bodies in a row.

The driver was beyond reach. The wreckage had him pinned. There are moments you know that trying means mutilation, not salvation. This was one of them.

I stood there, saw humming in my hand. Blood on my knees.

"I hate this part." Corey's voice was soft, cracked just enough to let the truth slip out.

I didn't say anything. Just stared at the ground. Because I hated it too. More than I wanted to admit.

After we'd done all we could, we loaded the bodies into the bed of another truck. The morgue was already full—stacked with the aftermath of too many impossible days. We sent them to the far side of the island, where temporary cold units hummed behind makeshift fences. Out of sight. Never out of mind.

The ride back was silent.

***

When we got to the hospital, I found the man from the flipped truck propped up on a cot, stitched and stabilized but looking hollowed out.

His eyes locked on me.

"Hey!" he called, voice thin but trying to be strong.

I walked over.

"Thank you for saving my life."

I nodded. "You're welcome."

He hesitated. His eyes searched mine. "Did the others... make it?"

I held his gaze a second too long.

"No. Not one."

His face didn't change. Not at first. Then something collapsed behind his eyes. He looked down at his hands. Opened his mouth like he was going to say something. Closed it.

Finally: "I'm sorry."

I didn't know what to say to that. So I just stood there.

"They were my friends," he said. Voice barely a whisper. "We were all on our way to work."

I put a hand on his shoulder. Didn't say anything. Because there was nothing to say that would make it better.

He nodded. Didn't look up.

I walked away. Left him with it. Because that's all you can do.

This job doesn't stop. It doesn't end when the last patient is loaded or the bodies are tagged. Most days, you're not a hero. You're just a witness. A pair of steady hands in a moment that's coming apart.

At best, you help someone survive. But more often, you're there for what happens after—the screaming, the silence, the unraveling. You're there to collect what's left and offer something that resembles closure—even if that's just a name, a body, or the confirmation that there's nothing left to save.

***

The rest of the day blurred. Back at the hospital, more patients. More wounds to clean, infections to treat, fevers to bring down. I moved through it like I always did—hands steady, voice calm, mind elsewhere.

By the time night came, I was running on fumes. Exhausted. Covered in grime and sweat.

I found a quiet corner. Pulled out my phone. Stared at it for a long time before I dialed.

I called her. Had to. My brain felt stretched too thin. After everything—mud, blood, body bags—I needed a voice that didn't come through a radio or scream across a field of broken metal.

She answered soft. Made me realize how far I'd drifted from warmth.

"Hey," I said.

"Hey. How are you?"

"Tired. Long day."

"Tell me."

So I did. Not all of it. But enough. The car accident. The bodies. The man who survived asking if his friends made it.

She listened. She always listened. No judgment. Just space to unravel.

Then, gently, she said it: "Maybe it's time to stop."

I didn't say anything.

"You've done enough," she continued. "Twelve years of this. You've planted your flag. The world is better because of what you've done. But maybe... maybe it's time to let someone else carry it for a while."

And for once, I didn't argue. I just sat there, her voice in my ear, and let it happen.

"I meant what I said before I left," I told her. "When I get back, we start planning the transition. Something real. Together."

She laughed—happy. Really happy.

But even in that warmth, there was something. A pause. A hesitation. She was quieter than usual. Not cold. Not detached. Just... dimmed. Like she was turning the volume down on herself, one notch at a time.

"I'm proud of you," she said. Soft. Almost too soft.

"You okay?" I asked.

"Yeah. Just tired. Miss you."

"I miss you too. I'll be home soon. A week. Maybe less."

"Okay."

Another pause. Longer this time.

"I love you," I said.

"I love you too."

And then we hung up.

I sat there for a long time after, staring at the phone in my hand.

Something felt off. She was quieter than she'd ever been. But I was exhausted. Covered in blood and dust. And part of me didn't want to know.

So I didn't press it.

I told myself she was just tired. That she missed me. That everything was fine.

We were happy.

Or we said we were.

And sometimes, saying it out loud is enough to make it feel true—until it isn't.

23

Twenty Minutes

A WEEK LATER, THE cargo planes began to arrive.

They came low and loud, cutting through the heat, tires hitting the runway hard. Big aircraft delivering relief by the ton—food, medical kits, water, and finally, generators. The shipment we'd been pressing for since the first hour on the ground.

By midmorning, we'd unloaded supplies from three aircraft. Three more sat at the edge of the tarmac, engines running. The heat was brutal. Hands burned. Shoulders screamed. Diesel and dust coated everything.

But everything was moving.

We'd found a rhythm, and rhythm is everything in disaster. Trucks staged in lines. Drivers we'd trained rolled forward without hesitation. Assignments passed hand to hand. Food to the church. Meds to the clinic above the ridge. Water to the camp where families had been sleeping under plastic for weeks.

By noon, the island was humming. Generators roared, bringing light and power to clinics, homes, kitchens. People ate for the first time in days. Phones lit up. Refrigerators hummed. Oxygen flowed. Light returned to places that had gone dark.

For the first time since we'd arrived, we weren't just holding ground. We were advancing it.

I felt it in every movement, every coordinated step. Dust hung in the air. Planes roared overhead. Trucks rumbled across the cracked tarmac. Radios crackled. For a few hours, the world felt exactly right.

I pulled my phone from my pocket. Grace. I wanted to share it with her. To hear her voice. To tell her about the generators, the trucks, the lines of people finally moving again.

No answer.

I sent a text: *Just checking in. Hope your morning is going well. Call me back when you get this. Love you.*

I put the phone away. Shrugged it off. Maybe she was busy. That's all it was.

More generators came off the planes—heavy, awkward, transformative. They meant more kitchens could run. More homes could come back to life.

An hour passed. I checked my phone again. Nothing from Grace. No read receipt. I called again. Voicemail.

Something didn't feel right.

I stepped away from the aircraft and dialed her father. He picked up immediately, voice light.

"How's it going over there?"

"We're slammed. In a good way. It's finally moving."

"That's great to hear."

"I can't reach Grace. Probably nothing. But something feels off."

"She was fine last night. Watched a movie. Dogs curled up with her. She sounded good."

I wanted to believe that.

"If you don't mind, maybe just check on her. Let me know she's okay? I got wrapped up this morning and forgot to call at our scheduled time. She might be upset. This might be her way of showing it."

"Of course."

I hung up and stood there a moment longer than necessary, listening to engines, watching men move crates. I told myself this was nothing.

***

Twenty minutes later, my phone rang.

Her father.

"Burke." His voice broke halfway through my name.

"What happened?" My chest tightened.

Silence.

"What happened?" I said again.

"She's gone."

I didn't understand. "What do you mean, gone? Gone where?"

Another pause. I could hear him breathing. Trying to get the words out.

"She ended her life."

The world didn't stop. That's what I remember most. The engines kept roaring. Men kept shouting. Trucks kept moving. The planes kept idling on the tarmac. Everything continued exactly as it had been.

But I wasn't in it anymore.

"Are you there?"

I couldn't answer. My throat had closed. My chest felt like someone had reached in and ripped everything out.

"Burke—"

I hung up.

The phone was still in my hand. I stared at it. Didn't remember ending the call. Didn't remember moving.

Around me, men carried crates. Someone shouted an order. A truck backed up, beeping. The sun beat down.

I dropped.

Didn't decide to. Just went down. Knees hit the tarmac hard. Hands flat against the grit and heat.

And I broke.

Not quietly. Not with any dignity. I sobbed—loud, ragged, the kind that tears itself out of your chest whether you want it to or not.

Men moved around me. I could see their boots. Hear their voices going quiet. Someone said my name. I didn't look up.

She was gone.

The woman I was going to marry. The one who understood the parts of me I'd never been able to explain to anyone else. Who listened like the words mattered. Who made me believe I could build a life outside of this work.

Gone.

Not taken by the storm. Not by accident. She'd ended her own life. Quietly. Deliberately. While I was here, thousands of miles away, coordinating generators and supply lines and telling myself everything was fine.

I stayed on my knees. Five minutes. Maybe ten. I don't know. Time didn't work right anymore.

My hands pressed into the gravel. Sun burning the back of my neck. Shoulders shaking. Breath coming in gasps that didn't feel like enough air.

Someone touched my shoulder. I shook them off.

Finally, I stood. Legs unsteady. Vision blurred. I walked to my truck without looking at anyone. Climbed in. Shut the door.

I drove.

No destination. Just away. Away from the noise, the engines, the men who didn't know where to look anymore. I kept driving until there was nothing around me but broken road and open sky.

I shut the engine off and sat there. Hands still on the wheel. Breathing like I'd been running.

The silence pressed in.

I leaned forward until my forehead rested against the steering wheel.

Here I was. Surrounded by destruction. Saving lives by the dozen. Coordinating food, power, water. Keeping people breathing. Keeping light in places that had gone dark.

And the one person who needed saving most had been alone.

While I was here doing what I'd always done, she was slipping away. And I was thousands of miles away, blind to it, useless when it mattered most.

I sat there until the sun started to drop. Then I drove back.

***

I extended my time on Abaco.

A week later, I flew home for her funeral.

The service was small. Her parents. A few close friends. Me.

I sat in the front row and stared at the casket. Dark wood. Polished. Closed.

They said things. I don't remember what. The words didn't land.

Afterward, they lowered her into the ground.

I stood at the edge and looked down. The casket disappeared inch by inch. Dirt hitting wood. Final. Permanent.

I didn't cry. I'd already cried everything out on the tarmac in Abaco.

Her mother hugged me. I felt her shaking. I stood there, arms at my sides, and let her hold on as long as she needed.

Her father shook my hand. Didn't say anything. Didn't need to.

Then I left.

***

I went back to the home we'd shared. Walked through rooms that still smelled like her. Coffee and lotion and the candles she liked to burn in the evenings.

Her mug was still in the sink. The book she'd been reading was on the nightstand, bookmark halfway through.

I packed what I could. Clothes. Photos. A few things her parents would want.

Then I locked the door and left.

***

I flew back to the island the next day.

I stayed another two months.

I found a house on the beach. Damaged but still standing. Windows cracked. Roof scarred. Salt everywhere. It was enough.

I slept there. Ate there. Stared out at the water when sleep wouldn't come.

The work continued. I moved through it like I was watching myself from a distance. Orders were given. Supplies moved. People were helped.

But I wasn't fully present. I was going through the motions. Muscle memory doing the work my mind couldn't focus on.

In the evenings, I went out to sea. Dove for my food. Conch. Lobster. Tuna. Moving slow and deliberate beneath the surface, where everything was quiet and pressure replaced noise.

The water didn't ask questions. It didn't care what I'd lost.

Down there, breath mattered more than memory. And for a while, that was enough.

I stripped life down to its simplest form. Work. Water. Food. Sleep.

Like a man trying to drink himself numb, except my bottle was routine and exhaustion.

I pushed forward the only way I knew how—by staying busy, by staying useful, by staying anywhere but inside my own head.

***

The death wish returned.

Quieter this time. But unmistakable.

When she was alive, I'd wanted to come home. After she died, I stopped caring whether I did.

The next deployment. The one after that. They blurred together.

Part of me wondered if one of them would finally be the mission I didn't walk away from.

And part of me didn't mind the thought.

I kept moving. Not because I was strong. But because stopping felt more dangerous than going on.

And that's where I spent most of my time. Thinking. Replaying moments. Missing signs. Wondering what I should have seen, what I should have said, where I failed.

The last time we spoke, she'd said she was proud of me. Her voice had been soft. Almost too soft.

I'd asked if she was okay.

She'd said yes.

And I'd believed her.

Because I was tired. Because I was covered in blood and dust. Because part of me didn't want to know.

So I didn't press it.

A miscalculated variable.

24

Dragon Eggs

ALMOST THREE YEARS HAD passed since her death.

By mid-2022, I didn't want another mission. I didn't want a war zone or an extraction plan. I wanted to know what remained when the noise stopped. I stepped away without announcement. I didn't disappear. I just let the current move on without me.

I went back to the state where I grew up. My parents were older now—slower, gentler. My mother was facing cancer again, and that sharpened everything. Conversations became deliberate. Time stopped feeling endless. I stayed because I wanted to, not because I felt obligated. That distinction mattered.

After that, I drove. No itinerary. Just a truck, a few tools, and the road. I slept in parking lots and pullouts, woke to gas stations glowing before dawn, listened to engines idle and wind move through empty places. I wasn't hunting answers. I was just paying attention.

Routine returned in fragments. Scripture in the mornings. Meditation when my thoughts got too loud. Archery for patience. Jiu-jitsu for humility. The range for precision. None of it was therapy. It was practice. Grief didn't disappear. It just became something I could see around.

I shared campsites with people I'd never meet again. We passed bottles, told stories we wouldn't repeat. The kind you only tell when there's no future audience. Honest ones.

Then, one morning, at a coffee shop thirty minutes from my parents' house, I met her.

She was Ukrainian. Early thirties. Dark hair pulled back, eyes alert and tired in equal measure. She sat alone at a corner table, laptop open, coffee untouched. Her son—six, maybe seven—colored beside her, fully absorbed in turning a blank page into something else.

I didn't plan to speak to her. I just did.

"Is this seat taken?"

She looked up, studied me briefly. "No. Please."

Her accent softened her English without dulling it. We started with safe ground—where she was from, how long she'd been in the States. She'd arrived eleven years earlier. I told her

I'd been doing humanitarian work and had recently stepped away. That earned a look of recognition.

"What about you?" I asked. "What do you do?"

"I'm a teacher at the local college."

Her son looked up from his drawing. "Do you like dragons?"

"I do."

He turned the paper toward me—a wide-winged creature in green and red, fire pouring from its mouth.

"That's excellent."

He smiled like it mattered.

"This is Sawyer," she said.

"Hi Sawyer, I'm Burke."

She extended her hand. "Natalia."

We talked for another twenty minutes. Easy conversation. Nothing forced. When she stood to leave, Sawyer waved.

"Bye!"

I waved back.

I didn't expect to see them again.

But I did. We kept running into each other. Same coffee shop, same time. A month later, she invited me to dinner.

"Nothing fancy," she said. "Just pasta. And Sawyer will talk your ear off about dinosaurs."

"Sounds perfect."

Her apartment was modest and orderly. Lived in. Sawyer showed me his room—rows of small cars lined up with care, a map of Ukraine pinned to the wall, cities marked with flags.

"That's where Babushka lives," he said, pointing to Pryluky.

Natalia stood in the doorway. "We call every week. The time difference makes it hard."

Dinner was easy. Sawyer talked about school and dinosaurs and whether pterodactyls counted as dragons. Natalia laughed more than she had before. Later, after Sawyer went to bed, we sat with tea and didn't rush to fill the quiet.

"Can I ask you something?" she said.

"Yeah."

"Why did you stop?"

"The work?"

She nodded.

I thought about it. "I lost someone. And I realized I'd been using the work to avoid dealing with it. So I stopped."

"How long ago?"

"Three years."

"I'm sorry."

"What about you?" I asked. "You said you came here eleven years ago. Alone?"

She hesitated. Then: "No. I had a partner. He... he ended his life. Four years ago."

The space between us shifted. Not with sympathy. Just recognition.

"I'm sorry," I said.

"Me too."

We didn't say anything else about it. We didn't need to.

***

One night a few weeks later, her car broke down outside town.

She called me. Embarrassed. Apologetic.

"I wouldn't ask, but—"

"I'm already on my way."

When I got there, Sawyer was asleep in the back seat. She looked exhausted.

"Thank you," she said. Not just for the car. For showing up.

While we waited for the tow truck, she leaned against my truck, arms crossed.

"You didn't have to come."

"I know."

"But you did."

"Yeah."

She looked at me. Really looked at me. "Why?"

"Because you called."

She smiled. Small, but real.

That's when I knew this was different.

***

By early spring, I'd been to her apartment enough times that Sawyer stopped asking if I was staying for dinner and just started setting three plates.

One evening, I showed up with groceries. She'd asked me to pick up beets for borscht, and I'd brought five different kinds, not knowing which one she meant.

She laughed when she saw them spread across her kitchen counter—golden beets, striped beets, regular red ones.

"You brought a beet museum."

"I didn't know there were options."

She picked up a golden beet, turned it over in her hands. "In Ukraine, we don't overthink beets. But this—" she held up the striped one, "—this is fancy. American fancy."

Sawyer wandered in, saw the spread, and immediately declared the golden beets were "dragon eggs." He lined them up on the windowsill like he was guarding treasure.

"See?" Natalia said, smiling. "Now we can't eat them. They're dragon eggs."

I watched her move through the kitchen—efficient, practiced. She taught me to chop without looking down, to taste as I went, to trust my instincts. The borscht took two hours. We ate it at midnight, sitting on her porch, bowls steaming in the cold air.

"My grandmother made this every Sunday," she said. "Even during the hard years. Even when there was nothing else."

"Why?"

"Because it reminded her that some things don't break."

She looked at me then. And I understood what she was really saying.

We were both people who'd lost a lot. But we were still here. Still making borscht. Still moving forward.

***

Sawyer's birthday came in late April.

Natalia invited me to the party. I almost said no. Parties weren't my thing. Kids weren't my thing. But I went anyway.

I brought a gift—a model kit. A dragon, of course. The kind you build yourself.

When Sawyer opened it, his face lit up.

"Can we build it now?"

"Maybe after cake," Natalia said, laughing.

But after the party, after the other kids left, Sawyer dragged me to the table. We spent two hours building that dragon, piece by piece. Natalia sat across from us, watching, smiling.

When we finished, Sawyer held it up like a trophy.

"Look, Mom! We made it!"

"I see. It's perfect."

He set it carefully on his shelf, next to the dragon eggs.

Later, after he went to bed, Natalia walked me to the door.

"Thank you," she said. "He doesn't let people in easily. Neither do I."

"I noticed."

She smiled. "But you're patient."

"I've had practice."

She kissed me. Just once. Soft. Then stepped back.

"Goodnight, Burke."

I drove home and couldn't stop thinking about it.

***

That night, I woke up panicked. Heart pounding. I'd had a nightmare about Grace.

I grabbed my phone. Almost called Natalia. Didn't.

Because I realized what was happening.

I was falling for her. For them. And that terrified me.

I'd lost Grace. I'd lost everything. And now I was building something again. And what if I lost this too?

I sat in my truck for an hour, hands on the wheel, trying to talk myself into walking away.

But I didn't.

The next day, I showed up at her apartment like nothing was wrong.

She noticed anyway.

"You okay?"

"Yeah. Just didn't sleep well."

She looked at me like she didn't believe me.

Later, when Sawyer was watching a movie, she sat beside me on the couch.

"You don't have to do this if you're not ready."

"Do what?"

"This. Us. I know you've been through something. I have too. And I know what it's like to be afraid of losing it again."

I looked at her. "How did you know?"

"Because I feel it too."

She took my hand.

"But I'm tired of being afraid," she said. "I'm tired of protecting myself from something that might never happen. So if you want this, I want it too. But if you don't, tell me now. Because Sawyer's already attached. And I can't let him get hurt."

I sat there for a long time.

Then: "I want this."

"You're sure?"

"I'm terrified. But I'm sure."

She kissed me. And for the first time in three years, the future didn't feel like a threat.

***

By early summer, I'd met her friends—other Ukrainian expats who'd known her since Alexei died. One of them pulled me aside: "Don't hurt her. Don't hurt that boy." I promised I wouldn't.

A few weeks later, I met her parents over video call. Her mother cried—happy tears. After, Natalia was quiet. "I'm afraid this is too good," she said. "That something will take it away."

I understood that fear better than anyone.

"I'm afraid too," I said.

She looked at me. "Really?"

"Every day. But I'm still here."

She leaned into me. "Then we're both brave idiots."

"Yeah. I guess we are."

***

Seven months after we met, I realized I wasn't just visiting anymore. I was staying.

One night, after Sawyer was asleep, we sat on her porch. Cold air, stars out, the world quiet.

"I want this," I said. "I want you. I want him. I want to build something here."

She looked at me. "You're sure?"

"I'm terrified. But I'm sure."

She was quiet for a moment. Then: "What if something happens? What if you get pulled back into the work?"

"I won't. I'm done."

"How do you know?"

"Because I have something to stay for now. I didn't before."

She leaned into me. "I'm afraid of losing you."

"I'm not going anywhere."

"You can't promise that."

"No. But I can promise I'll try."

She kissed me. And I meant it. I really did.

***

Three weeks later, Russia invaded Ukraine.

I woke to Natalia on the phone, speaking fast in Ukrainian, her voice breaking. When she hung up, her hands were shaking.

"What happened?"

"They're bombing Kyiv. My parents won't leave."

The days blurred after that. Calls. News updates. Half-plans that went nowhere. Sawyer asked questions she couldn't answer. One night, after he fell asleep, she sat at the table, head in her hands.

"I should be there."

She looked up at me. Eyes red. Exhausted.

"You know how to move in places like that. You've done this before."

I felt it. The pull. The same pull that had dragged me into every disaster zone, every war, every mission I'd ever taken.

The pull that had cost me Grace.

"Natalia—"

"I know what I said. I know I told you I was afraid of losing you to this work. I am. But my parents are trapped in a war-zone. People I grew up with are dying. And you have the skills to help."

She stood up. Paced. Tried to find the words.

"I don't want you to go. I want you here. Safe. With us. But I can't ask you to stay while my friends and family are under attack, and you could have helped them."

"You're asking me to go."

"I'm asking you to do what you think is right. And I'll hate it either way."

I stood up. Tried to think.

"If I go, I might not come back."

"I know."

"And if I don't go?"

She met my eyes. "You won't forgive yourself. And neither will I."

I sat back down. Closed my eyes.

I thought of Grace. Of the promise I'd made. Of Sawyer's dragon on the shelf. Of Natalia's hand in mine.

"Two weeks," I said. "I go for two weeks. Then I come home. And we build something here. We don't look back."

She nodded. "Okay."

"I mean it. Two weeks."

"I believe you."

But I could see it in her eyes. She didn't. Not really.

And I wasn't sure I did either.

***

The next morning, I packed.

Natalia watched from the doorway. Sawyer was still asleep.

"You'll call," she said.

"Every day."

"Promise me you'll come back."

I stopped. Turned to face her.

"I promise."

She stepped forward. Wrapped her arms around me. Held on longer than usual.

"I love you," she said.

It was the first time either of us had said it.

"I love you too."

She pulled back. Looked at me. "Then don't make me a liar for believing you."

25

Two Weeks

W E LANDED IN AMSTERDAM, then climbed onto a smaller plane bound for Romania. By the time we touched down in Bucharest, the team was already splitting. Half stayed to coordinate logistics. The intelligence guys headed to Poland to set up communications. The rest of us—the field team—climbed into battered vehicles and pushed through the Carpathians toward Ukraine.

The drive took hours. Snow clung to the pines. Cold air cut through cracks in the doors. We wound through switchbacks and valleys, the mountains silent and still.

Crossing into Ukraine at Siret, everything shifted.

Roads narrowed. Shadows deepened. Towns passed in eerie silence—empty buses, shuttered houses, dogs wandering without direction.

***

We arrived in Lviv two days after leaving Amsterdam.

Bomb sirens wailed from unseen speakers. The streets were full of people, but no one seemed present. They moved in slow, mechanical steps—dazed, as if their bodies had arrived but their minds were still catching up.

The invasion had been just over a week ago. The air hadn't settled yet.

Some stores were open, lights humming behind fogged glass. Others were shuttered tight, metal grates pulled down. Barricades of tires and sandbags squatted at street corners. Windows were boarded with plywood.

But cafes still poured coffee. Espresso machines hissed and clicked. People stood in loose lines for cigarettes, shoulders hunched, collars pulled up. A woman scrolled her phone. A man laughed at something I couldn't hear.

Life hadn't stopped. It had bent itself around the damage.

What would have been unthinkable a week earlier was already routine.

***

We weren't in Lviv to observe. We were there to connect, coordinate, assemble the pieces before moving forward.

We met soldiers on the outskirts, away from cafes and sirens, where buildings thinned and the ground felt less certain. Most were Georgian—veterans of other wars. Men who carried themselves with quiet efficiency, having learned not to waste energy on talk. Others had attached themselves to the Legion: Brits, Australians, a man from the Isle of Man. Each had a specialty. Each had already accepted where this road led.

From those meetings, the team grew. Some joined outright. Others supplied gear—medical kits, radios, armor scavenged from earlier fights. Higher-level contacts handled the paperwork: credentials, authorizations, documents that opened checkpoints. Quiet agreements that allowed movement through areas controlled by Ukrainian military and police. The difference between passage and detention.

It was methodical. Handshakes. Lists. Maps spread across vehicle hoods.

By the end of the day, the plan was set.

Our hotel sat just off the main square. A concrete building with an iron door.

Within an hour, we had comms up with the intel team in Warsaw. Maps came out. Gear followed. We laid everything on the floor—medical kits, batteries, plate carriers, night vision, encrypted radios—checking and rechecking. Not because anything had changed, but because repetition steadied nerves.

No one spoke much. Everyone wore the same expression: restless eyes, the early signs of fatigue.

Outside, a child struggled to pull a suitcase larger than his body. It tipped and scraped the pavement. His mother walked a step behind, clutching a stuffed bear.

I watched longer than I meant to.

That evening, we ate in a restaurant still open. Pizza, hot and greasy. Around us, people ate quietly. No one lingered. No one laughed too loudly.

Afterward, we returned to the hotel. Sleep came in fragments.

Before turning in, a local contact arrived with a thick stack of papers. Official stamps. Signatures. Authorization to move through checkpoints and secured zones. Our immunity. It wasn't armor, but it mattered more than most weapons.

He handed it over. No words. Just a nod.

***

That night, I called Natalia.

She answered on the second ring.

"Hey," I said.

"Hey. Where are you?"

"Lviv. We got in this afternoon."

"Are you safe?"

"Yeah. We're in a hotel. Gearing up. We move east tomorrow."

Silence on the other end.

"Natalia?"

"I'm here. Just... be careful."

"I will."

"Sawyer keeps asking when you're coming home. I don't know what to tell him."

I closed my eyes. "Two weeks. I'll be home in two weeks."

"Okay."

Another pause.

"I love you," I said.

"I love you too. Call me when you can."

"I will."

We hung up.

I sat there for a long time, staring at the phone in my hand.

***

By morning, another wave of missiles struck Kyiv.

We didn't hear the impact. But we felt it. The city slowed. Lines at pharmacies curled around corners. Soldiers checked weapons repeatedly, eyes lifting toward the sky.

War had entered the body.

That afternoon, I sat with a group of nurses displaced from Kharkiv. They'd arrived only hours earlier, carrying small bags and the stunned look of people who'd left everything behind too quickly to mourn.

One hadn't spoken in days. The others took turns brushing her hair, slow and methodical.

When I asked what they needed, I expected requests for supplies—antibiotics, gauze, painkillers.

Instead, one said, "A way to feel useful again."

I nodded. Gave them assignments. Small tasks—sorting supplies, organizing kits. Watched them straighten, shoulders squaring.

They didn't need much. Just a reason to keep moving.

***

That night, we packed the trucks. Trauma kits. Bandages. IFAK's. Food. Everything we could carry without slowing ourselves down.

Our destinations weren't hospitals. They were schools turned clinics, churches turned surgical bays, gyms lined with cots.

Maps from Warsaw guided us. First names circled in ink: Bucha. Irpin. Borodyanka. Russian-controlled. Civilians trapped. No power. No water. Executions reported in the streets.

The language was clinical. The reality wouldn't be.

Lying on a cot that night, I listened to the city. No explosions. No sirens. Just a thick, pressing quiet.

I thought about Natalia. About Sawyer's dragon on the shelf. About the promise I'd made.

Two weeks.

I told myself I'd keep it.

***

The next day, we left Lviv and pushed east, toward the front.

We wouldn't return for over sixty-three days.

26

Between Checkpoints

T HE NEXT MORNING, SIX of us set out for Kyiv.

The drive took seven hours. We passed roughly a half-dozen checkpoints, each one a careful exchange of papers and questions. Our credentials cleared the way. Being American helped—Ukraine is a U.S. partner, and that carried weight.

At the third checkpoint, a young soldier approached. Maybe twenty. His hands shook slightly as he took our documents.

He studied them longer than necessary. Looked up at us. Back at the papers.

"Where are you going?" His English was good but hesitant.

"Kyiv. Then east."

He nodded slowly. "East. Toward Bucha?"

"Eventually." I nodded.

He looked at me. Really looked at me. "That's where my family is. My parents. My sister."

I waited.

"If you see them..." He pulled a small notebook from his pocket, scribbled something, tore out the page. "Their names. The address. If you see them, tell them I'm okay. Tell them I'm trying to get back."

I took the paper. Folded it. Put it in my pocket.

"I'll try."

"Thank you." He handed back our documents. His hand was steadier now. "Be careful. It's bad out there."

He waved us through.

I never found his family.

***

At other checkpoints, we stopped to stretch. Let the engines cool. Let the cold air bite through the cab. Soldiers came over, leaned against the trucks, talked.

They spoke of recent ambushes. Scattered reports from the front. Comrades lost or wounded. Many had family with them in the fight—brothers, cousins, fathers. Some had been pulled from different lives entirely: mechanics, schoolteachers, shopkeepers. Now carrying rifles and responsibilities they'd never sought.

Some offered contacts—quiet suggestions for support farther east. Each expressed gratitude. Not for cameras or headlines. For our presence. For being willing to witness what was unfolding.

Between checkpoints, the landscape told the story.

Villages appeared like ghost towns—streets empty, homes shuttered or abandoned. A few residents remained, but they gave no hint of life to anyone passing. Windows dark. Doors closed tight. Even when smoke curled from a chimney or a figure moved across a yard, it was cautious. Deliberate. Fleeting.

Evidence of conflict was everywhere. Burned-out vehicles sat in ditches. Abandoned possessions littered the dirt. Scars from artillery fire marred fields and roads.

Yet traces of life persisted. A small farm still tended. A shop swept clean despite the absence of customers.

The quiet pressed down with every mile.

***

We rolled into Kyiv around 4 p.m.

The city was quieter than I expected. Streets almost empty. The usual hum of traffic subdued. The intel team in Warsaw had already lined up a place for us: a local hotel still operating in the heart of the city.

We unloaded gear, checked in, and claimed our rooms. The hotel was functional—nothing more. Narrow hallways. Small rooms. Beds that felt like they'd seen better decades. But it was shelter, and that was enough.

That evening, we had dinner in the hotel restaurant. Buffet style—grab what you wanted, pay a set price. The staff moved quietly, few in number but steady, doing their best under impossible circumstances.

We ate quickly. No one lingered. Outside the windows, the city prepared for night. Once the sun set, the lights would go out. Darkness was protection. Even a streetlamp could give someone a coordinate.

Our stay at the hotel would be brief. Becca, now part of our intel team, had secured a place just a few blocks away where we could establish ourselves for the week. Enough to catch our bearings before the real work began.

***

Before bed, a few of us gathered to run through the plan.

Packs were examined. Each piece of gear accounted for—what was present, what was missing, what could be improvised, what could fail. Every kit had to be instinctive. No hesitation.

Maps were spread across tables and beds. Routes marked. Alternate paths noted. Contingencies discussed—what to do if checkpoints were closed, if vehicles broke down, if enemy movements were detected ahead.

We ran through scenarios repeatedly. Vehicle breakdowns. Sudden ambushes. Civilians caught in the crossfire. Blocked roads. Hidden explosives.

The goal wasn't perfection. It was comprehension. So that when the moment came, decisions were executed with speed and clarity.

Tomorrow we'd source another vehicle—a point car, light and nimble, designed for speed.

Then we'd push farther east.

The meeting broke up around midnight. Everyone headed to their rooms.

I didn't.

I grabbed the satellite phone and climbed the stairs to the roof. The only place it worked reliably.

The air was cold. Clear. I could see the city stretching out in darkness below—no streetlights, no glow from windows. Just scattered shapes and shadows.

I dialed.

It was late—too late for her, early morning for me. She answered on the first ring.

"You're okay?"

"I'm okay."

"You're lying."

I smiled despite myself. "Maybe a little."

Silence. Not comfortable silence. The kind that means someone is choosing their words carefully.

"How much longer?" she asked.

"I don't know. Soon."

"You said two weeks."

"I know."

"It's been almost a week already."

I looked at the date on my watch. She was right. Five days since I'd left. Already slipping.

"I'm sorry."

"I know." Her voice was quieter now. "Sawyer drew you another dragon. He keeps asking when you're coming home."

"Tell him soon."

"I've been telling him that."

Another pause. Longer this time.

"You're not coming back in two weeks, are you?"

I didn't answer immediately. And that was answer enough.

"I want to," I said. "I'm trying."

"I know you are." She sounded tired. Not angry. Just tired. "But trying isn't the same as doing."

"Natalia—"

"It's okay. I understand. I do. But understanding doesn't make it easier."

In the background, I heard Sawyer calling for her. She said something to him in Ukrainian, soft and reassuring. Then she came back to the phone.

"I have to go. Be safe. Please."

"I will."

"I mean it. Come home to us."

"I will," I said again. And I almost believed it.

She hung up before I could say anything else.

I stood there on the roof for a long time, phone still in my hand, watching the sun rise over Kyiv.

Five days gone. Two weeks promised.

The math wasn't working.

27

Dug In

TWO DAYS AFTER ARRIVING in Kyiv, we got the call.

Bucha. Wounded trapped. Doctors overwhelmed. They needed someone to go in, collect the injured, deliver medical supplies.

We loaded the vehicle. Tourniquets, gauze, IVs, trauma kits. Not enough. Never enough. But it was what we had.

Four of us went: the driver, a doctor, a nurse, and me.

***

The drive took an hour. We passed three checkpoints before reaching the final one at the edge of Bucha.

The soldiers there didn't nod. Didn't wave us through. They stared like we'd already made a mistake.

One muttered, "Good luck out there."

The words hung in the cab after we drove past.

The road narrowed. Trees pressed close on both sides. Every bend could hide an ambush. Blacktop scarred with craters. Shrapnel scattered across the asphalt. Debris everywhere.

We kept the windows down. Glass was a liability—one explosion and it turned into shrapnel.

Small-arms fire cracked in the distance. Sharp. Scattered. Then silence. Then more fire.

The driver's hands stayed loose on the wheel. Gripping too tight meant slower reactions. You had to stay loose. Ready to swerve.

A few minutes later, heavier fire. Mortars. Artillery. Deep thumps you felt throughout your whole body.

No one spoke. The driver watched the road. The rest of us scanned—left, right, treeline, ahead.

Thirty minutes in, Bucha appeared.

No gates. No warning. Just wreckage.

Cars abandoned in the middle of the street. Doors open. Belongings scattered. Some burned to skeletons. Others riddled with bullet holes, metal curled outward.

Everything had been hit. Buildings. Walls. Cars. Street signs. Lamp posts. Every surface pocked with holes—small arms, shrapnel, heavy rounds. Nothing had been spared.

I'd been to war zones before. But I'd never seen destruction like this.

This wasn't combat. This was rage. Deliberate. Savage.

White fabric hung from antennas and mirrors. Pillowcases. Shirts. Anything that could signal surrender. They fluttered in the breeze.

Bodies lay on the road. On sidewalks. Near bicycles. Near groceries spilled on the pavement.

No uniforms. No weapons.

Civilians.

The driver kept moving. Stopping wasn't an option.

We passed a small team on the roadside, wiring anti-tank mines together. Six of them, nose-to-tail. Detonation cord disappearing into rubble.

The driver swerved wide.

One man stood, raised a fist. Others shouted, "Slava Ukraini!"

We kept driving.

***

We met the other vehicle in a small clearing down a narrow alleyway between buildings.

Two women jumped out. Opened the rear doors.

"You made it," one of them said. "The last car was not so lucky. It was hit by a mortar."

Inside: a man and a woman. Both bandaged. The man's face was burned. The woman's arm wrapped in blood-soaked gauze.

Our doctor and nurse moved fast. Helped them out. Guided them to our vehicle. Every movement careful—hands on shoulders, torsos eased onto seats, bandages checked.

The two Ukrainian women hugged the wounded. Whispered to them in Ukrainian. Tears streaked their faces.

The driver and I scanned the perimeter. Rubble. Treeline. Rooftops. So far, nothing.

Small-arms fire cracked all around us. Heavy artillery hit just west. We pressed ourselves against the wheel wells.

Once the wounded were secured in our vehicle, we started transferring supplies. Tourniquets. IVs. Trauma kits. Boxes of gauze. We moved everything from our truck to theirs.

The doctor and nurse helped the two women stack it. Packed tight. Stacked to the ceiling.

When it was done, the doctor turned to me.

"We're staying."

I looked at him. "What?"

"They don't have enough hands. We're staying to help."

The nurse nodded. "A few weeks. Then we'll catch up with you."

A few weeks.

I'd promised Natalia two weeks total. I was already five days in. And now the team was splitting, the mission extending, the timeline slipping further out of reach.

But I didn't say any of that.

"Be safe," I said.

The nurse smiled. Tired. "You too, amigo."

We shook hands. Then the driver and I got back in the vehicle.

Engines hummed. We pulled out.

I didn't look back. Didn't let myself think about the promise I'd made on a rooftop in Kyiv. Or the one I'd made to Natalia before I left.

***

We made it maybe two minutes before the shelling started.

The first impact hit behind us. Close. The blast hammered through the cab. Dust and debris erupted.

The driver swerved hard into a narrow alley. Pressed close to a concrete wall. Kept moving. Not fast enough to lose control. Not slow enough to become a target.

Another shell landed. Then another. The sound was deafening. Ringing in the ears. Chest rattling with each impact.

In the back, the wounded huddled together. The woman whispered something. The man held her hand.

Five minutes. That's how long we waited in that alley. Listening. Watching. Waiting for a gap.

Then—silence.

We moved.

Engine screaming. Tires sliding over broken pavement. Gravel and rubble spraying from the wheels.

Shells kept falling behind us. Not close enough to hit. Close enough to feel.

Every corner was a gamble. Every street could be blocked. Every shadow could hide a threat.

But we kept moving.

And then—we were out.

The shelling stopped. The road opened up. The same route we'd taken in now stretched behind us.

Crossing the final checkpoint felt surreal.

The same soldiers were there. Leaning against sandbags. Rifles slung. They recognized us.

One raised a hand. Brief salute. Not celebratory. Just acknowledgment.

***

The drive back to Kyiv took an hour. No one spoke. The adrenaline was still there, buzzing under the skin. Muscles still tight. Eyes still scanning even though the danger had passed.

Somewhere in the distance, a dog barked.

We passed streets scarred with fire. Windows shattered. Cars burned. Debris everywhere.

The hospital came into view. We pulled up. Engines idling.

We helped the wounded out. Careful not to jostle bandages. The woman's face was pale. The man's breathing shallow.

Hospital staff came out. Took them inside.

No one spoke. There was nothing to say.

After they were inside, we stood by the vehicle for a moment. The driver lit a cigarette. I stared at the sky.

Clouds thickened. Rain started. Fat drops hitting the pavement. Steam rising off the hot asphalt.

Tomorrow, we'd do it again.

28

22 Rounds

Here's the complete chapter with all the corrections:

For two weeks, we'd been visiting a small town on the southeastern front.

It started with a delivery. Medical supplies to the hospital. Food to the mayor's office. Standard run.

But we kept coming back.

The town was small. Maybe a few hundred people. Most lived simply—gardens behind every house, chickens in the yards scratching at the hard-packed earth. The men were fighting. The women and elderly stayed behind, keeping the town alive with work-worn hands and stubborn determination. The push from opposing forces was still far away, not yet an emergency for most.

One afternoon, the mayor invited us for tea. An older man, maybe sixty, with hands weathered from decades of farm work—callused palms, swollen knuckles, the kind of hands that knew soil better than paperwork. He sat us down in his office—bare walls, a single wooden desk scarred with use, a map of the region pinned with red marks that told stories no one wanted to hear.

"Thank you for coming," he said. His English was broken but clear, each word carefully chosen. "Most people leave. You stay."

The tea was strong. Black. Bitter but good.

We came back the next week. And the week after that. Brought food. Clothing. Small things to lift spirits—coffee that smelled like home, chocolate, cigarettes for the soldiers rotating back from the line with thousand-yard stares.

The people were kind. Honest. They didn't ask for much. Just wanted to know someone was paying attention. That they hadn't been forgotten in the war swallowing their country.

We grew attached to that town. To the old woman who always waved from her garden. To the children who'd gather around our vehicle, shy but curious. To the baker who'd slip us warm bread even though flour was scarce.

Then we heard it was under constant bombardment.

Russian forces were pushing through, trying to take it. The people were holding the line. Barely.

When the call came that morning—artillery hitting the hospital, civilians trapped—we didn't hesitate.

It was almost personal by then. We knew these people.

Four of us loaded into the BMW. Black. Matte. Unremarkable except for the faint HARP stencil on the side. Built for speed, reinforced underneath, windows that could take pressure but not direct hits.

We'd been counting artillery patterns for the past hour from our staging point. Twenty-two rounds per carousel. Eight minutes to reload. If we timed it right, we had a window.

From where we sat, our vantage point overlooking the valley, we could see one of the Russian battle tanks in the distance—a T-72 perched behind a concrete building, surveying the same place we were getting ready to go into. It's hard enough making these choices, but now that we could also see the opposing force made it a little bit harder and all too real.

That tank could see us too, if the crew was paying attention.

"Ready?" Driver asked, hands on the wheel.

We nodded. No one spoke. There was nothing left to say.

He hit the gas.

We kept the windows cracked—sealed glass could shatter from the pressure waves, turn into shrapnel inside the cabin.

Open windows gave the sound somewhere to go, let the concussive force pass through instead of building up.

Music played. Loud. Aggressive. Not for show. Just to keep focus sharp, to drown out the part of your brain that wants to calculate odds.

The road was torn up. Potholes from previous strikes. Debris scattered everywhere—twisted metal, chunks of concrete, things that used to be things.

We crossed the bridge at speed. The valley stretched out below us, dark and exposed, a kill zone if anyone was watching.

On the far side, we pulled hard left under a collapsed building. Concrete and steel twisted from previous strikes, rebar jutting out like broken bones. Not perfect. But enough.

SteDriver killed the engine. We sat there in sudden silence, counting.

Boom. A deep, earth-shaking sound that you feel in your chest before you hear it.

Pause.

Boom. Another. Closer this time.

Pause.

Boom.

Pause.

Reloading.

"Now," I said.

Driver fired the engine back up. We moved closer to the city, cutting the distance in half.

We found cover behind the remnants of a brick wall. The city was visible now through the smoke—buildings with walls blown out, roofs collapsed, streets cratered. Fires burning everywhere.

We sat. Waited. Counted again.

Boom. Boom. Boom.

The rhythm continued. Methodical. Deadly.

Pause.

Reloading.

"Go," I said.

Driver gunned it. This was the final push.

We slid to a stop against a building in the city itself, bumper nearly touching crumbled brick. The streets were torn apart. Artillery craters deep enough to swallow a man. Shrapnel everywhere—jagged pieces of metal embedded in walls, in pavement, in the sides of abandoned cars riddled with holes.

The smell hit immediately. Cordite. Burning rubber. Something else underneath—gas leaking, electrical fires, the acrid stench of destruction.

Doors opened. Danny and I moved into the street. The other two went to the rear, unloading medical kits and heading toward a building where soldiers waited, their faces pale through the doorway.

The air felt thick. Heavy. Every breath tasted like ash.

A man stumbled out of a burning house, smoke billowing behind him. Dazed. Blood on his face. Clutching a small dog to his chest like it was the only thing that mattered in the world.

Danny guided him toward the underground shelter, hand on his shoulder, voice low and steady. "Come on. You're okay. Come on."

Then I saw her.

A woman stepped out of the rubble. Or tried to. Her legs gave out almost immediately and she collapsed onto the broken pavement.

Her right arm was gone. Blown off at the shoulder. Blood soaked the front of her dress, dark and wet, pooling on the ground beneath her. Too much blood. The kind of blood loss that means minutes, not hours.

She looked up. Saw me.

"Help me."

Not a scream. Just a whisper. Barely enough to reach me over the distant rumble of artillery.

Her eyes locked on mine. Clear. Conscious. Terrified.

I ran.

She grabbed my legs with her left arm as I reached her, wrapping around me like I was the only thing keeping her upright. Maybe I was.

I knelt. Pulled a tourniquet from my kit with shaking hands. But there was nothing to tourniquet—the wound was too high, too close to the torso. I packed it with gauze, pressed hard, felt the warm wetness soak through. She didn't even flinch. Shock, probably. The body's mercy.

"We need to get you underground," I said, trying to keep my voice steady. "Medics are there. They can help you."

She shook her head weakly. I don't think she understood English. Or maybe the world had already narrowed to one thing: staying alive for one more breath, one more heartbeat.

Then I heard it.

The whistle. High-pitched. Incoming.

That sound—it's the sound that separates before from after. The sound that makes your blood go cold.

I didn't think. I lifted her and ran.

She was lighter than she should have been. Adrenaline, maybe. Or desperation.

Rounds hit around us.

Concrete exploded, chunks flying through the air. Asphalt erupted in black geysers. Buildings cracked and collapsed with sounds like thunder. The air compressed, released, compressed again, stole breath from your lungs.

I kept moving.

Her weight in my arms. My boots hitting pavement—left, right, left, right. The impact of shells behind me, beside me, ahead. Each one a hammer blow to the earth.

And then something happened that I can't explain.

It was like a path opened up. Not literally—the destruction was everywhere, constant, unrelenting. Explosions tearing the world apart in every direction. But as I ran, nothing touched us.

Shrapnel tore through the air inches away—I heard it whistle past my ear. Debris fell where I'd been a second before, cratering the ground. Explosions erupted on both sides, so close the heat washed over me. But not where I was. Not where we were.

It felt deliberate. Like someone had carved a line through the chaos and I was running it. Like invisible hands were guiding each step, each turn.

I don't know how else to describe it.

I've been in firefights before. I've been shelled before. I know what luck looks like—the random chance of being three feet left instead of three feet right when the round hits.

This wasn't luck.

This was something else.

My faith had been quiet for a long time. Years, maybe. Buried under too much violence, too many unanswered questions. But in that moment, running through a barrage that should have killed us both, I felt it again.

A presence. A hand. Something protecting us.

Not just me. Us.

I reached the underground entrance. A concrete stairwell leading down into darkness. Medics were waiting at the bottom, their hands already reaching up.

"Here! Here!" I shouted, though my voice was hoarse, raw from breathing smoke and dust.

I handed her off. They took her, moved fast, voices calm and professional. Trained hands assessing, stanching, stabilizing.

She looked at me one last time as they carried her deeper into the shelter. Her lips moved. I couldn't hear what she said.

I turned and ran back.

The dash back felt longer. Every step felt exposed. Like I'd used up all my protection on the way in and now I was on my own.

Artillery continued to fall. The rhythmic thunder of it. The ground shaking with each impact.

I reached the building where the others had sheltered. Pushed the door open, lungs burning.

Everyone stared. Not celebrating. Not relieved. Just silent. Faces pale in the dim light filtering through the broken windows.

Stephen broke it. "How the hell are you not dead?"

I didn't have an answer. I just shook my head, trying to catch my breath.

Inside, soldiers huddled in a stripped bathroom. Tile hanging loose from the walls. Pipes bent and broken. Eyes wide. Backs pressed against the wall like they could make themselves smaller, harder to hit.

My team sat in the adjacent room. Every impact outside sent dust sifting down from the ceiling. It looked like it was snowing inside the room—gray flakes drifting through the air, coating everything.

The building shook. Hard. A direct hit somewhere above us. That T-72 we'd seen from the vantage point—it was targeting this structure now. Methodical. Deliberate. Working its way through the building floor by floor.

"Come in, come in." One of the soldiers waved, voice cracking with fear and adrenaline. "Please. In here. Safer."

"It's okay," I said. Voice steady. Steadier than I felt.

I glanced at my team. One of them raised nine fingers. Pointed outside.

Nine rounds in. Thirteen left in the carousel.

We all understood. We'd been counting. Living inside the rhythm of the artillery. It was the only way to survive.

I spotted a dented coffee pot on a makeshift stove in the corner. Still warm.

"Coffee?"

Nods all around.

I poured into whatever cups we could find—chipped mugs, metal canteen cups, one cracked glass. Passed them around. Someone pulled out a plate of sliced sausage. Rationed. Precious. We ate. Drank. The coffee was bitter and perfect.

The building shook again. Plaster dust fell into our cups. No one cared.

I slid into a corner. Back against the wall. The cold concrete felt solid, real. I pulled out my phone. Signal was spotty but there.

Typed slowly, thumbs clumsy.

I'm in a bad spot. Done my best. Love you all.

Sent it to my family.

Then I put the phone away.

Nothing left to say. If this was it, that was enough.

Seconds stretched. Each one felt long. Dust continued to fall. Another round hit. Then another. The walls trembled but held.

The ceiling held. The walls held.

We held.

Then—nothing.

A pause. Too long to be coincidence. Too long to be reloading.

We looked at each other. Confused. Still breathing. Still whole.

I checked my watch. Past reload time. Way past.

Had they moved on? Run out of ammunition? Received new orders?

Didn't matter.

"Let's move."

"No! You will be killed! Please—do not go!" one of the soldiers shouted, grabbing my arm.

But we'd counted. We'd lived inside the rhythm. We knew the patterns. Waiting now was more dangerous. The next barrage could hit any second, or the building could finally give up and collapse on top of us.

We ran.

Out the door. Straight to the vehicle. Still intact, somehow. Tires still held air.

Engine roared to life. We moved before the door fully closed, before we'd even buckled in.

The city erupted behind us. Fire. Smoke. Debris raining down.

The bridge loomed ahead—our only way out. We crossed it at speed, the BMW's engine screaming, suspension bottoming out on the uneven surface.

Seconds after we cleared it, the first impact hit. The structure exploded behind us—concrete and steel lifting into the air in a fountain of destruction.

Driver didn't slow. Didn't look back. Engine screaming. Tires biting rubble and pavement and anything that would give traction.

We drove.

Outside the city, new arrivals were clustering. Clean vehicles. Cameras. Officials. Aid workers just arriving, asking questions, trying to understand what was happening.

We didn't stop. There was nothing to say to them. Nothing that would make sense.

We drove in silence. The city shrinking behind us in the rearview. Smoke still rising. The distant thunder of artillery continuing its work.

Back at base, we unloaded in silence. Gear stowed. Vehicle checked. Reports filed. The mechanical routine of it.

But none of us could stop moving. Restless. Wired. The adrenaline still coursing through us with nowhere to go.

I found myself outside, staring at nothing. The night was clear. Stars visible. It felt wrong somehow—that the stars could be beautiful while that town burned.

Stephen came out, handed me a bottle of water. We stood there together, not talking.

"She make it?" he finally asked.

"Don't know. Maybe."

He nodded. That was all there was to say.

For the next few days, we continued our rescue operations. Other towns. Other calls. The work didn't stop just because one town fell.

But that place stayed with us. The mayor with his careful English. The old woman in her garden. The children who'd waved. The baker's warm bread.

And the woman with no arm, looking up at me with those clear, terrified eyes.

I can't begin to explain how hard it is leaving places like this, whether it's a natural disaster or a man-made one. I find myself, more times than not, attempting to find reasons not to come home.

When you put so much emotion and feeling, care and love into an area by helping, by rescuing others, there's an attachment that takes place to the people, the area, everything. You become part of their story and they become part of yours. You carry them with you.

It's hard. It's more than hard.

And it costs a person a lot—mentally, physically, and for those waiting at home for your return.

But I also can't explain what it felt like running through that artillery barrage, carrying that woman, and knowing—*know-*

ing—that something was protecting us. That we weren't alone in that hell.

My faith had been quiet for so long. But it wasn't quiet anymore.

Sometimes God speaks in the silence of a church.

Sometimes He speaks in the thunder of artillery.

Sometimes He carves a path through the chaos and says: *Not today. Not yet. Keep running.*

I don't know if that woman survived. I hope she did. I pray she did.

But I know I was meant to try. I know I was meant to run.

And I know I wasn't running alone.

That's enough.

It has to be.

29

The Unavoidable

I FINALLY CAME HOME.

The plane touched down at LAX mid-afternoon. I moved through baggage claim, shoulders tight, scanning faces without thinking about it. Years of high-risk work had trained me to notice everything. That instinct didn't turn off just because I was home.

Then I saw her.

Natalia stood just beyond the railing. Calm. Steady.

We hugged. Not long. Not dramatic. Just grounding.

"You made it," she said.

"Yeah. I made it."

We loaded into her car and drove. No checkpoints. No artillery. Just traffic and sunlight and the hum of tires on asphalt.

I was home.

That first night, we sat on the porch after Sawyer went to bed. She'd made dinner—borscht, like the first time. Steam rose from the bowls. We ate in silence for a while.

"How was it?" she finally asked.

"Hard."

She nodded. Waited.

"I thought about you every day," I said. "About coming home. About keeping the promise."

"You came back. That's what matters."

I wanted to believe that. But even as I sat there, my mind was already somewhere else. Thinking about the people still in Ukraine. The work left undone. The calls I needed to make.

She was talking. I was nodding. But I wasn't really there.

***

The first week, I told myself I just needed time to adjust.

I'd check my phone constantly. Emails from the team still in Ukraine. Updates from intel. Requests for advice on routes, supplies, contacts.

I'd respond immediately. Middle of dinner. Middle of a conversation with Natalia. Middle of watching a movie with Sawyer.

"Can that wait?" she'd ask.

"It's important."

"So is this."

But I was already typing.

The pattern set in quickly.

I'd be physically present but mentally gone. Sitting on the couch, staring at my laptop. Planning. Coordinating. Staying connected to the work even though I'd left the field.

Natalia would ask me something. I'd look up, realize I hadn't heard a word.

"Sorry, what?"

"Never mind."

Sawyer would show me a drawing. I'd glance at it, say "that's great, buddy," and go back to my screen.

She stopped trying to talk to me about her day. Stopped asking me to help with Sawyer's homework. Stopped expecting me to be part of the life we were supposed to be building.

I didn't notice. Or I noticed and told myself I'd fix it later. After I handled this one thing. After I made this one call. After I finished this one task.

But there was always another thing.

***

Three weeks after I got home, she sat me down.

"This isn't working," she said.

I looked up from my laptop. "What?"

"This. Us. You came home, but you're not here."

"I am here. I'm sitting right next to you."

"No. You're not. You're in Ukraine. You're with the team. You're everywhere except here."

I closed the laptop. "I'm sorry. I've just been trying to help coordinate—"

"I don't care about Ukraine right now. I care about us. And you don't."

"That's not true."

"Isn't it? When's the last time you asked me about my day? When's the last time you spent time with Sawyer without checking your phone? When's the last time you were actually present?"

I didn't have an answer. She was right. I was slipping away, again.

"I thought you came home because you wanted to be here. With me. With us. But you didn't. You just brought the work with you."

"I'm trying—"

"No. You're not. You're doing the same thing you did before you left. You're choosing the mission over everything else. Over me."

She stood up. Walked to the window.

"I can't do this again. I won't."

"Natalia—"

"You need to leave."

I packed that night.

Kept my hands busy. Clothes into the duffel. Toiletries. Boots. The essentials.

I tried not to think about what was happening. Tried not to feel it. Just focused on the task. Pack. Organize. Move.

Natalia sat in the living room. Silent. I could hear Sawyer crying in his room.

I zipped the bag. Stood there for a moment. Then walked out.

She didn't get up. Didn't say goodbye.

I put the bag in the truck. Sat in the driver's seat. Stared at the steering wheel.

It hurt. More than I wanted to admit. More than I could let myself feel.

So I turned the key. Started the engine. Drove.

I didn't know where I was going. Just away.

The first week, I stayed in a motel outside the city.

I threw myself into the gym. Lifted until my muscles screamed. Ran until I couldn't think.

But at night, alone in that room, my mind wouldn't stop.

I'd lost her. Not because she stopped loving me. Because I couldn't stop being on mission long enough to actually be present.

I'd done it again. Different woman. Same pattern.

I didn't know how to explain that presence, for me, had always required effort that most people didn't need. That I wasn't choosing the mission over her. I just didn't know how to exist anywhere without a clear purpose anchoring me. I hadn't had language for that yet. I do now.

Grace died while I was doing the work. Natalia left because I couldn't stop doing it.

I told myself I'd learned. Told myself I'd changed. Told myself I wanted to live.

But I still didn't know how to live without the mission.

I decided to move. Not just to a new home. To a new place entirely.

I needed distance. From the city. From the noise.

My eyes had been opened to too much. I'd seen what people were capable of—the best and the worst. And coming home to a world where most people worried about traffic and Instagram felt unbearable.

I looked at a map. Found a small town in the mountains. Land. Space. Quiet.

I packed the truck and drove.

The place I found was small. A cabin. A barn. Fifteen acres.

I bought another dog for a hiking partner. An Alaskan Malamute. Smart. High-energy. Needed work.

Every morning, we'd walk into the woods. Miles. Just the two of us. The dog would run ahead, double back, check on me. I'd follow. Silent. Breathing.

The woods didn't ask questions. Didn't need me to be anything other than present.

I'd watch the dog move through the trees—alert, focused, alive. And I'd try to be the same. Just here. Just now.

Some mornings, I'd think about Natalia. About Sawyer. About the life I couldn't hold onto.

Other mornings, I'd just walk. Let the quiet settle in. Let the beauty of the place do what words couldn't.

It didn't fix anything. But it helped.

I kept working.

***

Over the next few years, I took four domestic operations. Wildfires. Floods. Missing persons. Search and rescue.

Nothing overseas. Nothing that required leaving for months.

But even when I was home, the mission was still there. In my head. In the background. Always running.

I also started working human trafficking cases. Quiet work. Important work. The kind that didn't make headlines but saved lives.

I'd show up. Do the work. Then go home.

I started riding again.

Built fences. Planted a garden. Fixed things that were broken.

I meditated. Prayed. Read scripture. Took care of myself in ways I'd neglected for years.

I was learning to be present. Learning to exist without constant urgency.

It was harder than anything I'd ever done.

Partly because I was rewiring patterns I'd had my whole life. The Asperger's diagnosis had come quietly, late, the way things arrive when you've spent decades compensating so well that no one thinks to look — including you. It reframed a lot. The relationships I'd lost. The way mission gave me structure that ordinary life never could. The reason I'd always been more comfortable in a disaster zone than a dinner party. I wasn't broken. I was just wired differently. And I'd spent forty-something years in a world that never told me that.

Because the mission had given me purpose. Identity. A reason to wake up.

And I still didn't know who I was without it.

Sometimes I think about that moment in Ukraine. Running through the barrage with the woman in my arms. How nothing touched us. How it felt like something was protecting us.

My faith had been quiet for years. But in that moment, it spoke.

I was given a second chance. Maybe a tenth chance.

And I'm trying not to waste it.

I didn't stop doing the work because I broke.

I stopped because I finally wanted to live.

But I'm still learning what that means.

I lost Grace. I lost Natalia. I lost years to a death wish disguised as purpose.

But I'm still here. Still breathing. Still trying. Still alive.

***

This morning, I woke before dawn. Let the dog out. Made coffee.

We walked into the woods. The air was cold. Crisp. The trees silent except for the wind moving through the branches.

The dog ran ahead, circled back, checked on me. I followed. Step by step. Breath by breath.

The sun broke over the ridge. Light filtered through the pines. The dog stopped. Looked back at me. Waited.

I stood there. Watching. Listening. Present.

Somewhere, people needed help. Somewhere, a disaster was unfolding.

But I was here. And for now, that was where I needed to be.

30

Finding Space to Live

I'VE SPENT MORE THAN a decade in disaster zones, in places where life and death breathe side by side. It changes you. Quietly, insidiously. Grief and fear leave marks—some necessary, some unavoidable. I've built walls, strong ones, in a feeble attempt to shield myself from loss. *Everything comes and goes,* I tell myself. And yet, peace doesn't come from avoidance.

Nature has been my refuge. Hiking until my legs burn, feeling the sun warm my skin, noticing the wind teasing through the trees, the flash of a bird diving across a canyon—each moment unique, each perfect because it cannot be repeated. Every child leaping through a minefield did it in their own way, precise and alive in its singularity. Each mother in the hospital ward tended her child in rhythms that belonged only to her. Even pain, grief, and loss have their own perfect logic, if only we can step back to see it. The world is full of unrepeatable moments, and noticing them is one of the few ways to hold onto what matters.

The call—the pull that brought me here—isn't theoretical anymore. It's alive. Every heartbeat, every step, every choice presses into me. Knowledge alone cannot explain it. I have to live it, answer it, or risk walking through the world half-awake, deaf to the pull that claims everything. Coping isn't avoidance; coping is carving space for life anyway, even when the ache is constant.

There's a subtle trap I've seen too many people fall into—the one where suffering becomes performance. Endless reflection, constant discussion, even therapy, can begin as tools, but slowly they take on a life of their own. The attention, the care, the validation—it feels good. People check in more. Others notice you more. And suddenly, the work of living becomes about proving the depth of your suffering. Pain can become your identity. I've seen it happen. I stay away from that trap. My life, my healing, comes from living fully, not narrating my suffering.

One of the strongest truths I've learned is that we create our own reality through the choices we make—and the meaning we assign to what happens to us. Nothing outside of us has the power to determine our inner life; it's our interpretation, our response, our awareness that shapes the experience. Out there, in the chaos of life-and-death situations, you can't control every outcome—but you *can* control how you respond, how you carry yourself, how you integrate the experience into who you are.

Responsibility is not blame. It is not shame. It is seeing clearly where your influence begins, where your action matters, and stepping into that space fully. In the field, every decision carries consequences. In life, it's no different. Suffering doesn't have to define identity. Trauma doesn't have to become performance. Your choices—how you respond, how you live, what you notice, what you let go of—shape the version of yourself that moves forward.

Another powerful insight is the influence of the stories we tell ourselves. The events themselves—the grief, the fear, the chaos—are raw, unchangeable reality. But the story you live inside, the narrative you carry, can either trap you in despair or allow you to move with awareness, courage, and gratitude. By consciously choosing how to frame your experience, you reclaim a power that is otherwise lost to rumination, self-pity, or endless replaying of trauma.

Presence is everything. Showing up fully, seeing what is true, acting deliberately, aligning your actions with your awareness—this is how you navigate both disaster zones and life at home. Observe without judgment, act without attachment, move without hesitation. Life isn't about perfection; it's about recognizing that each moment, each person, each experience is unique and unrepeatable—and responding with awareness, with courage, with full engagement.

The mind can only occupy one conversation at a time. If you let it linger on pain, grief, or fear, it will loop endlessly, dragging you down. You have to change the conversation. Move. Be active. Engage your body, your senses, your surroundings. Sitting still and dwelling is a trap, one that feeds anxiety and despair. Gym time is more than building strength—it's training the mind. I refuse to let the voice that says *I can't* or *I won't* creep in. I choose the opposite: *I can. I will. I must.* Even while knowing my limits, I act with deliberate focus and positive intention. That's how I accomplish what I do, why I can lead others, and why I can face loss without becoming lost.

Faith has been a quiet anchor. I don't claim to understand everything, and I don't question God's plan. I've learned to trust that there is a design beyond what I can see. Everyone wants to go to heaven, yet we grieve when others leave this world. I've stood in the dust, in hospital wards, in minefields, and felt that grief claw at me. Still—each life follows a path I cannot alter. Who am I to try? My work is not to control outcomes, but to act with presence, courage, and care, knowing some things are beyond my hands. These are my personal experiences, woven into the fabric of life itself, threaded alongside the lives and realities of others—the struggles they endure, the paths they walk, the beauty they witness. I move through the world not above it, but within it, part of the same unfolding story that carries everyone forward.

Gratitude is a quiet, fierce practice. Not the kind that demands perfection, but the kind that notices life in all its variations. The warmth of the sun, the subtle differences in a child's step, the way a mother lifts her child, the wind sweeping across a canyon—all perfect because they cannot repeat. Even after seeing the worst, these moments tether me to the present, reminding me why I move forward, why I engage, why I act. Gratitude doesn't erase grief—it sits beside it, a companion in awareness.

Through life, we change. Always. Every lesson, every moment, leaves its mark. Some see that change as negative, some as too small, too little. But if we take each lesson, reflect on it, learn from it, we begin to shape ourselves—the version we were meant to become. We live into that version, and it becomes our reality. Do not overlook who you were, and who you are becoming. Everything—every choice, every decision—forks the path to the life we ultimately create.

It is also powerful to become the observer of life itself. Not just noticing, not just moving, but stepping back and letting the world move through you. Shutting off internal conversation—the judgments, the fears, the replay of pain—and simply taking it in. Every sound, every light, every breath, every motion, experienced fully but without attachment. You watch the world as it is, not as you want it to be, not as you hope it will be. You see the perfection in each fleeting movement, each moment unrepeatable and complete.

I move forward. Always forward. I lean into the deliberate, tangible, present moments—the steps, the breaths, the quiet hours, the effort, the observation. I let grief coexist with wonder, loss coexist with love. Survival is not numbness. Survival is presence. Deliberate. Full. In a world fragile, fleeting, perfect in ways we barely notice. In that presence, I've found clarity—not the peace the world promises, but a recognition that even pain is perfect, and that living fully, despite it, is the only choice that matters.

Live. Notice. Grieve without becoming grief. Love without fear. Move through the world fully awake, even when it hurts. Life does not wait for courage—it *is* courage, moment by fleeting moment. And in that, even the smallest heartbeat becomes enough.

And if that's not enough, reach out to me. Say hi. And we'll talk.

Epilogue

IF YOU'RE READING THIS and you recognize yourself in these pages—if you've spent years running toward disasters, if you've lost relationships because you couldn't turn off the mission, if you've used the work to avoid dealing with your own life—I want you to know something.

You're not alone.

And you're not broken.

But you might be running from something you haven't named yet.

I was.

For twelve years, I told myself I was doing good. Saving lives. Making a difference. And I was. But I was also running toward death because I didn't know how to live.

The work gave me purpose. Identity. A reason to exist. But it also hollowed me out. Made me incapable of the thing I wanted most: a normal life with people I loved.

I lost two women I loved. Not because they failed. Because I couldn't stop being on mission long enough to actually be present.

I came home from Ukraine after three months. Three weeks later, Natalia asked me to leave. Not because she stopped loving me. Because I was physically there but mentally still in the field. Still planning. Still coordinating. Still on mission.

I couldn't turn it off.

And it cost me everything.

I'm telling you this because I wish someone had told me earlier: the mission will always be there. There will always be another disaster. Another person who needs help. Another place falling apart.

But your life matters too.

The people who love you matter too.

And if you can't turn it off—if you're always planning the next deployment, always checking your phone, always ready to respond—you're not serving anymore. You're running.

I learned that the hard way.

I'm still learning.

I'm here now. In the mountains. Doing domestic rescue work. Search and rescue. Human trafficking cases. Work I can do without leaving for months. Work I can do without destroying myself in the process.

Some days are good. Some days the ghosts come back. But I wake up most mornings grateful to be alive.

That's progress.

If you're still out there, running, I hope you figure it out before you lose everything.

Because the work will take everything you give it.

And it will always ask for more.

Burke Bryant has spent over a decade responding to disasters around the world. As a humanitarian responder specializing in high-risk extraction, he has worked in Haiti, Indonesia, Ukraine, the Bahamas, and dozens of other crisis zones. He is a two-time Presidential Lifetime Achievement Award recipient for his humanitarian work.

For years, the work was everything — his identity, his structure, his reason to move. It was also all he knew. And while he was fully present in every disaster zone, everything outside the mission quietly fell apart. Relationships. Stillness.

The ordinary life that kept slipping out of reach. After twelve years, his body and mind finally forced him to choose — and he chose to live.

Now based in the mountains, he does domestic rescue work — search and rescue, missing persons, human trafficking cases, firefighting — and is learning what it means to serve without destroying yourself.

Burke speaks to organizations about mission obsession, burnout, sustainable service, and leadership under pressure. His talks draw from real experience in disaster zones and offer honest lessons on resilience, presence, and choosing life over constant urgency.

He lives with his two dogs, rides horses, tends a garden, surfs, and continually grapples with what it means to exist as a person, beyond the mission.

If you'd like to reach out, say hello, or just share a thought:
www.burkebryant.com / www.harprescue.org
Social: @burkebryant

Read more from Burke Bryant